To the U-2 brotherhood, all 1116 of my brothers and sisters.

You are my heroes.

Acknowledgments

I would like to thank my wife for encouraging me to pursue my dreams. She has been a big inspiration throughout my entire career. I would also like to thank the U2PS brothers for answering all my questions. A special thanks to Rick Bishop, Don Yu, and Andrew Saleh for their ideas, editing, and help with the technical aspects of writing this book.

I am indebted to Bette James for her meticulous editing of this project. She can make a writer look good.

Map of North Korea

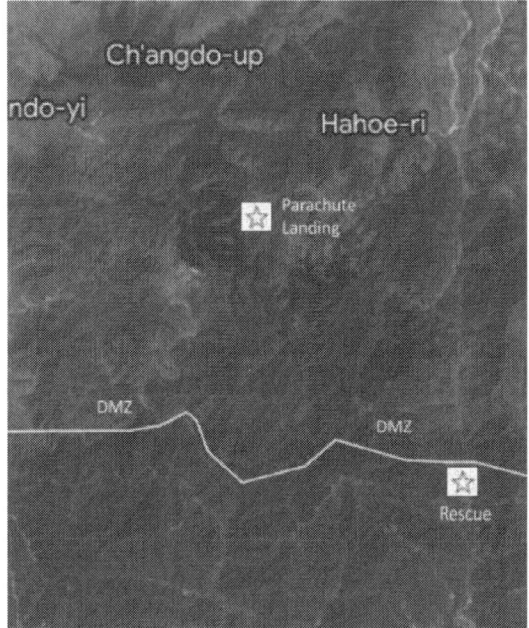

Ejection and Rescue Sites

Chapters

Chapter 1 - Korea
Chapter 2 - The Flight
Chapter 3 - The Ejection
Chapter 4 - The Plan
Chapter 5 - The Encounter
Chapter 6 - The Rescue
Chapter 7 - Going Home

Introduction

Imagine a late summer night in July, where Lt. Colonel Dan Preston is wrapping up a grueling day at work. But Lt. Colonel Preston's "office" is unlike any other—he's a pilot of the Lockheed U-2 aircraft, soaring above 70,000 feet along the highly fortified DMZ that divides North and South Korea. As night falls, missiles begin to fly. He faces a daunting enemy, fighting to survive alone and deep behind enemy lines. With no immediate help from his country, Lt. Colonel Preston must navigate back to safety.

"Dragon is Down" offers a riveting glimpse into the secretive world of operating the renowned U-2 spy plane, a feat achieved by only 1116 pilots. What's it like to operate in an environment where a person can freeze to death in less than a minute and perish in 30 seconds without oxygen? There's no room for error in this high-altitude realm.

Multiple U-2s take to the skies worldwide daily, earning the nickname "Dragon Lady" for their crucial role in averting conflicts. During the Cuban Missile Crisis, a U-2 pilot sacrificed his life while providing vital intelligence that unveiled the truth about Soviet intentions. The stakes are always high for the Dragon Lady pilots as they confront the profound responsibility of their missions.

One day, the mighty engines of the Dragon Lady might fall silent, but that day is not today. Buckle up for a glimpse into a world where the sound of freedom echoes through the sky.

CHAPTER 1

Korea

I couldn't open the gate; none of the keys seemed to work in the lock. I could hear the chomping of the beast's three-inch teeth smashing together. He was possessed and would not stop until I was his next victim. The nauseating smell of an old rotten carcass in his belly blew past my hair each time he snapped his jaws together. My heart was racing; this was it. The metal bars made an eerie screeching sound as they began to bend. The beast was winning. I could not afford to look back; I didn't have the time.

Fumbling with the keys, I figured I had thirty to forty seconds left before it was over. The outcome was not a pleasant thought. The image of being eaten alive pulsed in my mind. Nothing in the world could be worse than feeling a predator rip my flesh apart. How had I gotten myself into this mess? I couldn't remember. Precious seconds passed, while my survival lay on the other side of the locked door. My whole body was shaking, making it hard to hold the keys. I couldn't remember which keys

I had tried before. It was useless; too many keys with too little time. I wouldn't even get to see my kids grow up. What would my wife do?

Suddenly, I heard the phone ring. Who would be calling me at a time like this? I couldn't afford to answer it. If I did, I would lose scarce seconds to find the right key. Just then, a claw sliced me from behind, sending warm blood flowing down my lower back. The beast was almost upon me.

I heard more ringing. Something in my mind told me to answer the phone. But how could that help? How would that help my situation? Two more rings. The pull to answer the phone was strong. I reached for the phone and said, "Hello." There was no answer, only a dial tone. My senses started to return. I realized it wasn't the phone ringing but the alarm clock going off. As I was reaching for the clock, the beeping stopped. The clock was gone; somebody had yanked the electrical contraption out of the wall.

"Lt. Colonel, wake up!" a high-pitched voice yelled. "It's time to go to work."

My fuzzy world started to become clearer. I blinked my eyes several times, trying to adjust them to the overhead light. "What are you doing here?" I asked.

Captain Brady Jackson laughed and said, "You overslept, and your alarm clock has been going off for the last two minutes."

Shaking my head, I let out a small chuckle. "Sorry about that," I replied, pulling myself up to a sitting position on the bed. Sweat trickled down the middle of my back from my clammy skin. I took a deep breath as the grogginess from my brain started to fade away.

"Colonel, is everything okay?" Brady inquired in his humorous tone.

"Yeah," I replied. My body felt like it had just come out of a boiling pot of water. Glancing at the floor, I saw my alarm clock upside down. The electronic window, which usually showed the time, was pitch black. "What time is it?" I asked.

Rotating his left wrist, Brady replied, "It's four-forty in the morning."

Puzzled, I asked, "What happened to my alarm clock?"

"Sorry about that," Brady responded, placing the clock back on the nightstand. "I couldn't figure out how to shut it off, so I yanked the damn thing out of the wall. It's a noisy son of a gun."

Rubbing my eyes with the palms of my hands, I stated, "I shouldn't have watched that Jurassic Park movie last night. I knew I was going to have nightmares."

"Oooh, I love that movie," Brady said. "Especially the part where...."

I heard nothing Brady said as I was still collecting my thoughts. My sleeping habits had been off since arriving in South Korea two days earlier. I always had difficulty adjusting my internal clock when traveling westbound from Northern California.

I stood up and headed to the bathroom as Brady was still discussing the movie. "Just give me a couple of minutes to get myself together. I'll meet you in the car," I said, interrupting Brady.

"Roger dodger boss," Brady responded, heading out the door of my room.

Dang, I thought to myself. When I got back last night, I didn't even lock my door. It was good that I didn't have to fly for two more days, as I was still a walking zombie. Today, I had only to preflight the plane for Brady's 7 a.m. takeoff and then hit the books to brush up on the flight procedures in Korea.

Five days ago, my superior in the United States had informed me of my deployment to Korea for a two-week stint to fill in for the Operations Officer who had taken emergency leave. The sudden military orders surprised my wife and me, necessitating a rush to attend to last-minute arrangements at home. Though I had hoped to coast through my last few months before retirement, the military had a different plan in store for me. Nonetheless, I endeavored to maintain a positive outlook; at the very least, I would have the opportunity to fly one final operational mission along the DMZ before embarking on a new career path.

Captain Brady Jackson, a bald African American man originally from Philadelphia, suffered from a medical condition called Madarosis, resulting in the loss of all body hair, including his eyebrows. Brady enjoyed playfully claiming that he'd had had a full head of hair before flying the U-2, attributing his baldness to flying at high altitudes close to the sun. There was shock on people's faces as they were engrossed in his storytelling ability, only to be followed by his mischievous wink. Seeing new interviewees' relief when they realized it was all a joke was always a priceless moment for Brady and all who were listening close by.

Brady's passions in life were clear cut: Philly baseball, Philly cheesesteaks, and airplanes, although not necessarily in that order. His intellect was as keen as they come, leading to his recruitment into the U-2 program four years earlier. Thanks to his razor-sharp mind, Brady quickly ascended to the Standard and Evaluations program. The Stan/Eval pilots were the best pilots in a squadron and were entrusted with administering checkrides to all the pilots. His photographic memory allowed him effortlessly to recall the intricate workings of every system on the U-2 aircraft. Observing his intellect in action was akin to watching Da Vinci paint the Mona Lisa. Numerous pilots, including seasoned U-2 aviators, frequently sought him out when confronted with perplexing queries. Brady would provide the solution, sometimes even specifying the exact page number within seconds. Conversely, this often made us average pilots feel inadequate as we had to consult the manual for answers.

I spent a full minute staring at my reflection in the mirror, trying to come to terms with the changes in my 41-year-old body. The telltale signs of aging were becoming more pronounced—the dark circles under my eyes, the streaks of gray in my once jet-black hair. My wife had jokingly started calling me "Old Salty," a nod to the accumulating salty-colored streaks that have appeared over the last couple of years. It was easy to notice the loss of muscle tone in my arms as well. Gone were the days when a trip to the gym was a given; now, as a senior pilot, responsibilities outside of flying took precedence. Meetings and a myriad of other duties kept me busy all hours of the day. My body was the one to suffer. Keeping in shape was becoming increasingly challenging, especially with early morning wake-up calls.

After hastily brushing my teeth, I stepped into the shower, trying to be as efficient as possible. The shower was like a quick drive-through car wash—in and out in mere minutes. Dressed in shorts adorned with little airplanes, a not-so-subtle reminder of my love for flying, I couldn't help but remember my wife's words about needing good-looking shorts in case of an unforeseen hospital visit. Next, I put on a white T-shirt with matching socks, and then I slipped into my green flight suit. All in all, it was a very comfortable get-up for the heat of the summer months. Last but not least, I slid on my black boots with a no-tie speed lace lock. I appreciated how the Air Force had perfected the art of practical footwear in combat boots. In less than five minutes, I was out the door, feeling refreshed and ready for whatever the day had in store.

I hurried down the stairs of our two-story dormitory, which housed all the temporary duty pilots. As I stepped outside, I saw Brady sitting in a striking blue Ford Mustang equipped with a police light bar on top. At first glance, it was hard to distinguish our Mustang from the police cars back in the States.

In the U-2 program, the Mustang serves as a chase car during the takeoff and landing phase to assist the pilot flying the aircraft. Unlike other Air Force planes, the U-2 is incredibly hard to land. The challenges of landing the U-2 are twofold. First, the limited visibility out of the front windshield makes it difficult to find visual references. Second, the U-2 was designed with only two wheels – one in the front and one in the back – whereas other military aircraft typically have three wheels to ensure stability on landing. The decision to forego the extra landing wheel in the U-2 design was to reduce the weight, allowing the plane to fly higher. As a result, pilots have to delicately balance the U-2 on the two landing wheels while using the ailerons on the wings to keep the plane level during the landing phase.

The U-2 aircraft approaches the runway threshold at approximately 90 mph and 10 feet in altitude. The backup or mobile pilot driving the Mustang maneuvers the car to match the aircraft's speed and position themselves directly behind the plane as both plane and car speed down the runway. The mobile pilot then announces the height of the aircraft's front main wheels above the runway. The flying pilot attempts to stall the aircraft two to three feet above the ground to execute a successful landing. Misjudging the altitude could result in damaging the aircraft or even veering off the runway. After a prolonged nine-hour mission, receiving altitude calls from the mobile pilot provided a comforting reassurance.

Tracking down a U-2 in a Mustang also had its challenges, especially when dealing with the hazard of standing water on the runway. The Mustang was prone to spinning out in heavy downpours on non-grooved runways while attempting to catch up with the faster U-2. Many chase car pilots had terrifying experiences of high-speed spinouts, almost feeling their lives slip away as they skidded off the opposite side of the runway.

The U-2's landing struggles over the years earned it the moniker "Dragon Lady." Pilots faced a daunting choice—they could either battle the "Dragon" or gracefully dance with the "Lady," but they could never do both simultaneously.

The Dragon has claimed numerous pilots over its operational life. Landing the aircraft is an intense and aggressive endeavor, with pilots forcefully slamming the control yoke to its limits to keep the aircraft stable. However, the satisfaction of mastering the Lady is enough to keep seasoned pilots in the program while enticing new recruits to take on the challenge. Flying the Dragon Lady demands nerves of steel; it's been known to push even the best pilots to the brink, eliciting moments of doubt and tears of frustration.

The interview process is also no easy task. First, you have to make it through a rigorous selection process before even getting a chance to interview for the job. If the commanders like you after a series of interviews, you can get a shot at flying the Dragon Lady, consisting of three flights, each with around 15 landings. What makes it even more challenging is the fact that the aircraft has no hydraulic controls. Instead, the controls are operated by cables running throughout the fuselage. Maneuvering the aircraft requires sheer physical strength, and after 15 landings, pilots' arms will involuntarily twitch from the immense effort.

Those who show improvement in each flight might receive a job offer. Still, some pilots are offered the position only to decline due to its daunting challenge.

However, being a U-2 pilot has its downsides. Flying a single-seat aircraft means enduring long, lonely missions with no one to talk to for up to nine hours. Additionally, being confined in a tight cockpit while wearing a space suit allows for only a little movement, adding to the physical and mental strain of the job.

Pilots in the program have to master a delicate process in order to take care of their bodily needs. To urinate, they have to skillfully operate their space suit, with female pilots needing to wear a special diaper and male pilots having to use a condom-like apparatus. After inflating the suit, pilots open a valve to allow liquid waste to pass through a clear tube to a holding tank. This process can take up to 50 miles to complete, and any malfunction would lead to a very uncomfortable situation.

There were no procedures for defecation in the space suit. A pilot has to endure extreme discomfort if he can't wait until landing. The embarrassment of admitting the need to defecate and subsequently terminating a mission early always brings up serious concerns from the brass. Pilots who can't hold it has to provide a case of beer as compensation for clean-up, and their names are inscribed on a special trophy for all to see. It's another challenging and unique aspect of the job, and one that is not without humor!

As we made our way to the base dining facility for breakfast, the air hummed with friendly chatter. A few military personnel strolled casually ahead of us, showing no particular rush to eat the same daily buffet. Yet, for us U-2 pilots, the morning routine was different. We had the privilege of choosing a high-protein meal before each flight, and steak and eggs were usually the top preference.

Once inside the cockpit, strapped into the space suit, a U-2 pilot's sustenance options are limited to "tube food." These pre-blended rations, prepared years earlier, come neatly packaged in a silver aluminum tube with a gold food-grade liner to keep the contents fresh. Each five-ounce tube, about the size of a hot dog bun, offers flavors like Bacon and Eggs, Sloppy Joe, and Chili, which can be heated to bring out their flavors if that is possible.

In the lower-left corner of the cockpit, a small compartment was designed to heat the special food. A pilot can activate a special timer to shut off the heater at a predetermined time. Due to the pilot's insulated gloves, it is difficult to discern whether the food is hot or cold by touch alone.

To consume the food, the pilot screws on a rigid white straw-looking probe to the top of the tube and inserts the other end into a small aperture near the mouth of the helmet. By gently squeezing the tube, the pilot can cause the food to flow through the probe and into his mouth. However, since the probe is not transparent, there is no way to see the food moving closer to your mouth. The only way to test the temperature of the food is by placing a small amount on the tip of the tongue.

Squeezing the tube too forcefully could lead to an unexpected rush of scalding hot food, potentially causing discomfort or even necessitating spitting it out into the faceshield. Thus, opting for a hot meal during a flight always came with a higher degree of risk.

Served chilled, the more appealing options like Applesauce, Peaches, and Pears are much better choices. All the tube food had a familiar taste, reminiscent of the rations served during the Gulf War, since the same company that produced Meals Ready to Eat (MREs) manufactured our tube food.

I was excited as I stepped up and placed my order for a medium-rare steak and three scrambled eggs accompanied by toast. I observed intently as the cook grilled a slender strip of steak, just a tad thicker than a slice of bacon. Initially, I estimated a minute per side would suffice, but I was mistaken. Regardless of how anyone ordered their steak in the military, it invariably emerged well done. The military chefs executed their duty meticulously, mindful of the consequences of undercooking any meat and the potential harm it could cause their fellow airmen. Adhering to strict regulations, all meat products had to be prepared well-done.

Upon receiving our trays of food, I insisted on covering the bill for both of us, considering I had overslept. Surprisingly, the total amounted to a mere $5.87, including our refreshing orange juices. The military charged an unbeatable price, a perfect way to start the day after oversleeping.

After breakfast, we drove to our squadron near the flightline, set back behind the control tower. Korea was known as the Land of Morning Calm, but sometimes, there was too much calm as the morning fog meandered in. The Jin-wi River snaked around the flightline at Osan Air Base like a serpent guarding its inhabitants against all enemies. While highlighting the mysticism of the Korean peninsula, the river could wreak havoc with the early morning launches. On some occasions, Mother Nature would delay or even prevent the Dragon from flying.

Several large hangars housed a pair of Lockheed U-2s and were barely visible through the haze. The aircraft used for today's mission had already been pulled out of the hangar and positioned in the middle of the ramp. Three portable airfield lighting generators lit the area, cutting through the fog. Contractors and military personnel moved about like ants accomplishing their preflight tasks on the airplane. Everything was synchronized backward from the time of the launch. Life Support, oxygen, fuel, and electronics personnel had specific times to be at the aircraft and complete their jobs. It was a well-oiled machine, as long as there were no issues.

The Dragon Lady was designed and built in the 1950s by the Lockheed Skunk Works program. The program, led by Kelly Johnson, created many top-secret military aircraft in the Nevada desert, away from prying eyes. Even though the Dragon Lady had many hours under her wings today, she still had a fire in her belly. She could fly over 70,000 feet above you without you ever knowing. She could track you down, watch you with her precision cameras, and then listen to your phone conversations. If the Dragon Lady didn't know who you were, she could run a voice match and soon find out. Seventy years after her birth, she was at the top of her game. Many newer creations tried to knock her off her perch, but all have failed.

We stepped out of the car and took in the mysticism surrounding the old bird. Excess oxygen gently bellowed out of her fuselage, adding to the foggy conditions. Without the ramp lights, she would have been invisible in the darkness. Her 104-foot albatross-like wings connected to her fuselage. Two inlet nostrils provided air to her lungs. Buried deep inside her belly, she carried 17,500 pounds of pure power. All the Dragon wanted to do was to fly.

The aircraft's sleek black exterior was accentuated only by a striking red outline of a cat's face on her tail. We were famously recognized as the "Black Cats," a surviving unit from the Vietnam War repurposed for operations in

South Korea. People were always curious about our work, but we referred to ourselves as the Black Cats, which usually ended any further questioning. Our missions were highly classified, and serious trouble could follow those prying for too much information. Few dared to press questions beyond our Black Cat response.

As Brady entered Ops, he made a beeline for the Intel briefing to stay updated on any last-minute changes that may have occurred overnight.

I made my way in the opposite direction, heading toward the office of the commander, Lt. Col. Grover Jeffries, who led the Black Cats Squadron. As I entered his office, I noticed the strong display of his Alabama roots. Behind his desk, a larger-than-life picture of Bear Bryant and a photo of the University of Alabama football team dominated the wall decorations. Grover, hailing from Enterprise, Alabama, had the physique of an NFL linebacker. Despite his Marine-like appearance with a high and tight haircut, flying ran in his veins.

Being a squadron commander was a challenging job for a pilot. Although it was a great honor, a pilot had to focus more on administrative work than flying. The majority of Grover's time was taken up by the non-flying issues within the squadron. The commander's job resembled running a business, with the complexity of dealing with a multitude of diverse personalities.

Approaching him, I asked, "How are you holding up, boss?" Despite holding the same rank, I always paid the utmost respect to those in charge of a squadron. My job, a much easier task, was to keep the flying part of the squadron running smoothly.

He shook his head wearily as he picked up a stack of papers from his desk. With his thick southern drawl, he said, "I've got more headaches than Tylenol can handle. I'm on the verge of firing a Lockheed technician for defrauding the government, and my Korean subcontractors are a month behind in installing the fire suppression systems in the hangars. On top of that, I have to write four commendation medals for my maintenance troops before tomorrow night's banquet."

I couldn't help but feel empathy for him. A usually strong and capable man, he now seemed utterly defeated. It was a familiar look I'd seen on many Air Force commanders where flying became a secondary job. I knew there was only one way to lift his spirits. "Would you like me to schedule a low sortie for you?" I offered.

"That would be fantastic, my friend," Grover replied with a hint of gratitude in his voice.

Smiling, I added, "Would Friday work for you?"

"That's perfect. How about 10 o'clock after the mission bird launches?" he replied.

"Consider it done," I said, giving him a wave as I left. I didn't want to take up too much of his time, worrying that he might assign me some extra administrative tasks.

Entering the operations room, I saw Brady wrapping up with the mission planner and the Intelligence Officer. "Are there any updates I should be aware of?" I inquired.

He shook his head and said, "Nope, nothing's changed from yesterday. The weather might be a bit iffy for takeoff, but they're optimistic it will clear up by launch time."

"Great," I replied. "The boss wants to schedule a low sortie on Friday. Can you mobile for him?"

"Absolutely. It's about time he got up in the air. He's been working way too hard," Brady remarked. "Well, I'm off to Life Support to suit up."

"Roger, I'll start the preflight after I add the boss to the schedule. Any requests on your cockpit setup?" I inquired.

As Brady prepared to leave the room, he instructed me on his preferred setup, "Drinks on the right, food on the left, and could you please grab the latest newspaper for me to read?"

"Of course," I responded as I opened the scheduling book to jot down Grover's 10 o'clock takeoff with Brady as the mobile pilot.

Saying goodbye to the mission planner, I collected Brady's flight kit and headed to preflight the plane.

As I passed through the door to operations, I caught sight of "Oscar," the black cat who served as the squadron's mascot. Oscar was extremely well fed, and nobody dared taunt him. No one knew what number this particular Oscar was. Years earlier, one Oscar accidentally jumped up on an electrical transformer and met his demise while shutting down the power to the squadron.

Passing the secretary's desk, I glanced for any newspapers lying around. No military newspapers were immediately in sight, but I did find a couple of Korean newspapers on the cleaning lady's cart. One particular paper caught my eye: a multi-page listing of the latest Korean obituaries, along with photos, in their native language. Oh, he will like this, I told myself, shoving the paper into Brady's flight kit. It was the best I could do on such short notice, and Brady deserved the best.

As I strolled from the operations building to the aircraft, I saw the jet and noticed the absence of any other personnel. This indicated that it was my turn to conduct the preflight check. The backup pilot for a U-2 mission preflighted the aircraft. The primary pilot had only to jump into the cockpit, start the engine and go. I was eagerly anticipating my late afternoon flight in two days.

I ascended the five steps up to the cockpit and carefully conducted a swift safety check to ensure the ejection pins were installed. I placed Brady's flight kit in its designated spot on the right side near the seat. Taking note of the location of the beverages and snacks, I ensured everything was arranged correctly. Then, I jumped into the cockpit and began my preflight. I meticulously cross-referenced the latitude and longitude coordinates on the navigation computer with the ones listed on the map boards. A single error in the navigation data could potentially lead to a serious international incident. After confirming that everything was in perfect order, I exited the cockpit. The entire cockpit preflight was completed in less than six minutes.

As I descended the stairs, I began my familiar walk around, starting from the front of the aircraft, scanning above and below all the aircraft surfaces to ensure no fuel, hydraulics, or oil leaks were present. In addition, I checked all the flight controls to confirm they moved smoothly with no binding. I had developed a deep fondness for this old bird, finding it a challenging yet incredibly rewarding aircraft to fly. Despite being designed many years ago, it held a special place in my heart. The aircraft's unique capability to carry sensors to the edges of space made it cost-effective and highly valuable, preventing any serious consideration of phasing it out.

The underbelly and wing pods were adorned with an array of antennas, each serving as a conduit for its intelligence equipment. It never ceased to amaze me how, with each new overseas trip, another antenna appeared on the aircraft's underbelly. Overseas, the aircraft was transformed from a mere surveillance plane to a cutting-edge platform for the latest high-tech gadgets and innovations.

My attention was abruptly diverted when I spotted something unusual. The left aileron inexplicably snapped upward as I was about to grab hold of it. It was a disconcerting sight, stirring suspicions of unauthorized meddling with the controls while I was accomplishing my preflight routine.

I shifted my gaze toward the cockpit, hoping to catch a glimpse of the person inside. However, the canopy obstructed my view, leaving me with no sign of anyone in the cockpit. My curiosity stirred. It occurred to me that someone moving the opposite aileron could trigger a response on the aileron on my side of the plane. Yet, as I scanned beneath the fuselage, I found no trace of anyone on the other side of the aircraft. It was undoubtedly perplexing.

I decided to pause my walk around to investigate this issue. Striding toward the front of the aircraft, I noticed that the cockpit was empty and no personnel were near the wings. I wondered what could have caused the aileron to move on its own.

Meanwhile, the crew chief was occupied off to the side of the aircraft, engrossed in his tasks with the air cart. I glanced toward the hangar and noticed a contractor or technician fiddling with a small silver box on a nearby table, then disappearing inside the dimly lit hangar. Due to his distance from the aircraft, it was implausible that this individual could have been in the cockpit.

Puzzled by my dilemma, I climbed the aircraft stairs and peered into the empty cockpit. My attention was drawn to the "Master Caution" light, which was illuminated with the autopilot activated. Below the Master Caution light, the "DownLink Control" light was also illuminated. This was–unusual—I had never witnessed the DownLink Control light illuminated before. While airborne, a pilot had the capability to relinquish control of the aircraft to ground operators, although few pilots would willingly do so.

It dawned on me that the only way the DownLink Control light could be activated was if someone in the cockpit had specifically selected it. Curiously, no one else was around. Leaning in, I reached over and deactivated the DownLink Control light, in turn causing the "Master Caution" light to extinguish and the autopilot to disconnect.

As I descended the stairs, I carefully maneuvered around the six-inch air hose connected to the aircraft's fuselage and made my way to the crew chief. Whenever there was an issue with the aircraft, seeking out the crew chief was always the best course of action. Before takeoff, the Dragon Lady was their property, and it was terrible protocol if there was an issue with the plane and the crew chief was not informed.

After the crew chief removed his black ear protectors, due

to the loud noise of the air cart, I relayed my issue to him and requested assistance locating a Lockheed technician. I could sense the relief in the young man's demeanor upon learning that there were no issues with any of his aircraft systems.

I was hopeful that the Lockheed technician would be able to shed some light on the situation. Shortly after, the crew chief reappeared with a middle-aged representative from Lockheed. The man had blonde hair and was dressed in shorts and a loose-fitting Hawaiian shirt, giving the impression that he had just arrived from the beach to join the Lockheed team at Palmdale in Southern California. He embodied a laid-back California style, except for his distinctive pair of geeky black glasses that stood out against the rest of his appearance.

As the crew chief carried on with his duties, I greeted the Lockheed representative and learned his name was Ted Ross. Walking up the steps to the cockpit, I recalled every detail, with the aileron snapping upward and seeing the DownLink Control light on in the cockpit.

After spending a minute scanning the instruments, Mr. Ross turned to me and inquired, "Are you certain nobody else was in the cockpit?"

"No, I was the only one here, except for the crew chief, but he was at the back of the plane by the air cart," I responded.

The technician adjusted his glasses thoughtfully, taking in all the information I had provided. He reset several switches in the cockpit and then took a deep breath before stating, "I can't seem to find anything wrong. If you'd like, I could run some diagnostic tests, but it would take about an hour."

An hour's delay was simply not feasible, especially since we didn't even know what the problem was. I gritted my teeth and replied, "No, let's launch the sortie and run the diagnostics after the recovery." Sometimes, these "Gremlins," as everyone called them, just appeared and then vanished as quickly as they came.

"Alright, I'll have my partner run some tests after the recovery this afternoon," he informed me.

"Sounds good," I responded. I made a mental note to brief Brady about what I had witnessed so he'd be prepared if he encountered a similar issue while airborne.

As I returned to the other side of the aircraft, I completed the rest of the preflight checks with no issues. Before heading to Life Support to confer with Brady, I took one final scan of the airplane to ensure she was ready. During my short walk, I also reminded myself to inquire after the launch if any of the other pilots inside operations had encountered a similar issue before.

As I approached the Life Support area, I saw Brady sprawled out in a recliner chair with his sunshade pulled down. He seemed to savor his last leisure moments before heading to work as a U-2 pilot. It was a serene and contented time for him, and I hesitated to interrupt it.

After putting on a black headset, I asked, "How's everything going?"

"Great, just enjoying some downtime," Brady replied, lifting his sunshade visor.

"I wanted to give you a heads-up," I began. "While conducting the walk around, I noticed the DownLink

Control light and the autopilot were on. I've never encountered anything like that before. So, I punched off the DownLink Control light, which extinguished, along with the autopilot disconnecting. I called the Lockheed tech over, and explained everything to him and even he was stumped. We couldn't duplicate the problem."

"Was someone in the cockpit while you were doing the walk around?" Brady inquired.

I knew that question was coming as Brady's brain worked at warp speed. "No, that was my initial thought—that someone accidentally activated the switch. However, no one was near the plane during my preflight," I explained. "So that's all we know. If you see the light come on during flight, just deactivate it. We'll run some software diagnostics after you land."

"Roger," Brady said, giving me the thumbs up.

Feeling reassured that I had given Brady all the pertinent information I had, I bid him farewell and headed back to the operations building. Upon entering ops, I noticed Grover was nowhere to be found, with only the mission planner busy planning the next day's flight. I then turned on the power to a row of UHF aircraft radios in their charging stations by the wall.

Newly trained U-2 pilots are required to come to Korea for their first deployment. The reasoning is, during the orbit along the DMZ, the pilot is in constant communication with the mobile pilot in ops throughout the entire route. If they encounter any issues, they can swiftly call for assistance. Immediate communication with another pilot is incredibly valuable. The experience and confidence a new U-2 pilot gains in Korea helps them when flying other missions throughout the world, where they might be out of radio contact. No U-2 pilot wants to make the wrong decision as that might lead to a global news event, something nobody wanted.

Before leaving, I took one last look around the room and grabbed one of the black radios from its charging station. After pressing the transmit button and saying "Test. Test." into it, I heard the echo in the room, giving me confidence that my radio was functioning correctly. If needed, I could also communicate with operations while I was out with the airplane. I then grabbed the keys to the mobile car and headed out.

I parked the mustang in front of the aircraft, providing a clear view of any activity around it. Approaching 30 minutes before takeoff, Brady emerged from the Life Support building, accompanied by a technician carrying the 100% liquid oxygen container used for transporting the suited-up pilot to the aircraft.

After carefully guiding Brady into the snug cockpit, the Life Support technician fastened him into the seat kit and attached the parachute. Once Brady was securely in place, the technician disconnected the portable oxygen and ventilation systems from his suit.

The final tasks for Life Support included removing the five safety pins from the ejection systems, parachute, and scramble handle. In the event of an emergency on the ground, the pilot, with one action, could pull the scramble handle which would automatically disconnect Brady from the seat. Pulling the scramble handle saved critical time if one needed to get out of the cockpit in a hurry.

I observed the Life Support technician presenting the five safety pins to Brady and then to me for confirmation, I ascended the steps and meticulously surveyed the cockpit. I was the last line of defense in case there was any oversight in strapping a pilot into the cockpit. Satisfied that everything was in order, I signaled Brady with a thumbs up, and he reciprocated the gesture. Reaching across the top of Brady's helmet, I grasped the canopy locking lever and firmly closed the canopy while Brady secured it from inside the cockpit.

Returning to the car, I activated the overhead flashing lights, indicating that the airplane was prepared for engine start. Then, I shifted the car into drive and cautiously maneuvered around the aircraft to ensure no latches were open or additional equipment had inadvertently been left too close to the aircraft. After completing my checks, I keyed the radio and announced, "Mobile's up."

With all preflight checks complete, Brady signaled the crew chief to activate the external air cart, supplying vital air to the engine blades to initiate rotation. With the engine RPM reaching the required level, Brady smoothly moved the throttle from the cutoff position to idle. As the throttle settled into the idle position, the igniters sparked while fuel was meticulously sprayed into the combustion chamber, resulting in an immediate ignition. The Dragon Lady, as always, let out a resounding roar as she came to life, signifying the beginning of another day of vigilant surveillance over the world's threats.

As the engine purred gracefully, the crew chief and his team hurriedly detached the aircraft's external air hose and electrical power cable while securing the final two latches before carefully moving a safe distance away from the aircraft. I gave the "all clear" call to Brady for taxi.

After receiving taxi clearance, Brady gently increased the power, commencing the gradual journey toward the runway. Maneuvering the aircraft cautiously, Brady taxied at a walking pace, mindful of the necessity that the two orange semi-flexible steel outriggers, or as the pilots called them "pogos", were positioned beneath each wing for taxiing.

Positioning the car strategically behind the aircraft, I ensured that I had a complete view of everything happening in front of the plane. It was a breathtaking sight to behold—an aging aircraft getting ready to soar through the skies once again. In just two days, I would be the one trying to tame the Dragon. It was hard to control my anticipation.

After being cleared for takeoff and lining up on the runway, I meticulously drove down the centerline for a quarter of a mile in front of the aircraft to scan for any obstacles that could impede its takeoff. Then, I circled back to observe the ground crew removing the pogo safety pins. Once the wings flexed on takeoff, the pogo wheels would fall harmlessly on the runway. With the ground crew safely clear, I circled the aircraft one final time and signaled to Brady that everything was good to go for takeoff with a thumbs-up.

Brady gradually advanced the throttle to 80% momentarily to check the engine instruments before releasing the brakes and applying full power. The Dragon Lady surged forward as she gained speed down the runway. Just six seconds after releasing the brakes, her wings flexed upward, allowing for more airflow as she prepared to take flight. A second later, the pogos fell off, tumbling down the runway. The Dragon then gracefully lifted her nose toward the sky, stopping at a 35-degree nose high pitch before vanishing into the low fog enveloping the base. It was a truly remarkable sight to witness.

With the aircraft launched, I escorted the maintenance personnel off the runway after they collected the pogos and drove back to operations.

Being the backup pilot meant long stretches of downtime once the aircraft had taken off. I decided to brush up on the operational procedures for my flight in two days. It had been quite a while since my last mission in Korea, and even though I was reasonably confident that not much had changed, I wanted to ensure that I was well-prepared.

About twenty minutes later, I heard Brady's laughter coming over the radio. "Established in the orbit, and whose brilliant idea was the newspaper written in Korean?" he jested.

"Apologies for that screw up. It was the only one I could find on such short notice. I thought the pictures would be interesting," I explained.

There was a brief silence before Brady retorted, "Is this an obituary newspaper?"

"Sorry about that. I'll do better next time. I'm still getting the hang of things around here," I chuckled.

"Getting the hang of things, my foot. I'll have my day," came Brady's witty retort.

"Roger that," I replied, placing the microphone down as Major Terry Heinz entered the room.

Catching only part of the exchange, Terry inquired, "What did you do?"

"Nothing much," I answered. "Just a mix-up with the newspapers."

"Yeah, right," he chuckled. "Sorry, I missed it."

Terry strode into ops, ready to prep for his upcoming mission the following day. His takeoff was set for noon, while mine was pushed back to 4 p.m. the day after. The higher-ups believed staggering the takeoffs would catch the North Koreans off guard, although none of us were entirely convinced. That was the prevailing rumor, nonetheless.

Terry's journey in the Air Force began years ago when he enlisted as a mechanic, diligently working on fighter jets. However, he grew tired of being on the sidelines and decided to become an officer, eager to take flight instead of merely repairing aircraft.

Standing tall at 6'1" with a distinct southern drawl, the Texan boasted thinning brownish hair with a noticeable bald spot at the crown of his head. Hailing from San Antonio, he had a penchant for playing dice in the squadron bar, often challenging any unlucky pilot and relieving him of his money. His signature move was to exclaim, "Baby needs a new pair of shoes," as he vigorously shook the dice in the cup before slamming them down on the bar's surface. If he won, his follow-up line was always, "Baby's got some new shoes." It felt like a line from a movie, though no one, not even Terry, could recall its origin.

More than a few unsuspecting pilots found themselves indebted to him for hundreds of dollars, debts likely never to be paid. Yet, for Terry, it wasn't about the money; winning was the only thing that truly mattered to him.

At the squadron bar, amidst the excitement of dice rolling, the floor was covered in discarded peanut shells. For years, pilots had relished the tradition of cracking open salted peanuts in their shells, only to casually toss the empty remnants onto the floor. The combination of peanut shells and spilled beer created a rather unpleasant and pungent mess, which had to be swiftly cleaned up before any personnel arrived the next day. The arduous challenge of cleaning up the mess after a lively evening was the job of the newest pilots to solo the Dragon Lady. In addition to that painful task, the crews also had to ensure they never ran out of peanuts and beer, or their squadron mates would give them an earful. The "Bar-Maids," as they were often called, would get replaced only when the next crop of pilots flew the Dragon by themselves.

As I prepared for my upcoming flight, I carefully delved into the intricate procedures while Terry reviewed his flight paperwork for the following day. Although studying the procedures felt tedious, it was a necessary task. First and foremost, I meticulously went through all the emergency protocols. Fortunately, due to the U-2's high altitude, we could rely on gliding back to base in the event of an emergency.

Next, I devoted time to reviewing the regulations concerning the "Blue House," where the President of South Korea resides. The challenge arose from the fact that, unlike the American "White House," the location of the "Blue House" moved wherever the President did. It was crucial to ensure that we never flew over the residence of South Korea's leader, as any violation would have serious consequences. Although we could adjust our flight path if given prior notice, sometimes crucial information got lost in translation through communication channels.

After familiarizing myself with all the necessary procedures, I shifted my focus to the latest intelligence on the threats posed by North Korea. The intelligence information revealed the existence of two confirmed SA-2 missile sites in North Korea. One was situated approximately 30 miles north of the DMZ on the western side of the country. At the same time, the other was positioned on the eastern side near the Sea of Japan. Furthermore, the map highlighted six areas indicating the potential presence of mobile SA-2 sites. In addition to these, two permanent SA-5 sites were located roughly 50 miles north of the border. Although I didn't observe any changes in the missile locations from my previous missions in South Korea, I noted that the latest intelligence was only a week old.

With my eyes feeling tired and the excitement of the morning launch wearing off, I carefully placed the Intel binder on my desk. The mid-day blues were hitting me as I leaned back in my creaky office chair. Closing my eyes, I took in a nice relaxing deep breath.

Terry interrupted my moment of peace with his characteristic chuckle. "Welcome to Korea and the battle with jet lag. Feeling hungry? I'm ready to grab some lunch," he said, with a big smile.

"Absolutely, anything to take a break from this tedious studying," I replied, eager for the distraction.

Terry quickly gathered his navigation boards and paperwork and stuffed them into his flight kit. "Let's get out of here," he said, brimming with energy.

"Where do you want to go?" I asked, ready to go along with whatever his taste buds required.

Terry instinctively suggested, "Let's stay close since you have the mobile today and walk over to the Black Cat Lounge."

I had almost forgotten about the cozy Black Cat Lounge nestled around the corner from our building. It had been quite some time since I had last dined there. Picking up the portable radio, we set off for the short stroll to the restaurant.

The Lounge, often referred to as the "Loungee" by the pilots, was named after our squadron. It was a popular spot among U.S. service members working near the flightline. Despite its small size, the restaurant was renowned for its exceptionally delicious, authentic Korean cuisine.

As I reached for the Loungee door handle, I mentally prepared myself for the assault on my senses that waited inside. With the door wide open, I inhaled deeply. The first scent to greet me was the familiar aroma of pungent, spicy red pepper, a staple in almost all Korean dishes. This pepper had been forbidden in the U.S. for many years and was only recently given the green light to be imported. Alongside the red pepper, I detected the distinct fragrance of Kimchi, a beloved Korean classic. This sour, vinegary dish comprised nothing more than cabbage soaked in red pepper and fermented underground for weeks. While most Americans turned their noses up at the dish, the

Koreans savored it like a sweet treat. Lastly, the alluring scent of Bulgogi, a thinly sliced meat dish marinated for hours and served over white rice, floated by my nostrils, completing the enticing aromatic medley.

Approaching the counter, I perused the menu above, contemplating which familiar dishes I might indulge in. Bibimbap, a long-time favorite, came to mind. This dish consisted of a delightful mix of vegetables and rice, topped with a fried egg.

In an attempt to be gentle on my system, I decided to have Black Cat soup. Terry agreed with my choice. This renowned restaurant specialty was made with a rich variety of various sea creatures. The ones poking their heads above the liquid surface were a mystery to all. The only item I recognized was the transparent noodles. It was an unspoken agreement among the patrons not to inquire too much about the ingredients.

As I surveyed the scene, I caught sight of the restaurant owner, affectionately known as Mama-san. Standing barely over four feet tall, with black hair and a well stained apron, she expertly wielded a meat cleaver while commanding her young Korean staff. They hurried about, making sure not to incur her displeasure. I could only imagine how her husband avoided her wrath while fleeing from the menacing meat cleaver. She was a true force to be reckoned with, and none dared to provoke her ire.

As Mama-san's eye caught the sight of Terry and me, she abruptly ceased her Korean tirade. A forced smile crept onto her face, accompanied by a slight tilt of her head as a gesture of deference. We returned the nod, although fear was more prevalent than genuine respect.

Pointing a finger at me while squinting, she spoke in broken English, "I remember you GI. You have been gone long time."

"Yes, I have," I replied.

"What you have today?" she inquired, her tone growing more serious.

After glancing at the menu above her, I responded, "We'll both have Black Cat soups today, non-spicy, and two Cokes."

Curling her lips, she asked, "You no want Kimchi today?"

"No, I'm going to pass today. I just got in the country and I'm trying to let my system get adjusted," I stated firmly.

Raising an eyebrow, she said, "Okay, you go sit down. I'll make soup for you." With that, she abruptly resumed yelling in Korean at her staff, turning to wink at us, subtly conveying that she ran a tight ship. The land of Morning Calm only went so far in the Loungee.

As we turned to find two open seats, I expressed my gratitude to her in Korean, using one of the three words I knew in her native language. Once seated, I briefed Terry about the preflight issue I had encountered with the DownLink Control light. I also updated him on the Lockheed representative who planned to conduct some tests after the plane landed. Terry suggested contacting the Link ground personnel upon our return to the squadron for further insights.

Shortly afterward, Mama-san served us each a grand, colorful bowl that could easily satisfy any grown man for the entire day. Instead of simply placing the food on the table and returning to the kitchen, she waited for our approval of her culinary creation. With chopsticks in hand, I gathered a generous portion of noodles and an assortment of unidentified seafood. The dish was hot in temperature and spices, causing me to smile and nod while attempting to manage the fiery sensation in my mouth. After successfully tasting the first bite, I tried to convey my approval with an Italian-inspired exclamation of "Perfecto."

In response, Mama-san smiled and remarked, "I like you, GI. Next time, I'll make you Kimchi." With that, she resumed her duties in the kitchen, exuding a rugged exterior as she went about her work. Despite her formidable demeanor, I sensed that she harbored a kind-hearted nature deep within her.

The meal was delicious, although I was sure it would overwhelm my stomach for the rest of the day. Terry and I engaged in easy conversation, as I had no urgent tasks to tend to back at the squadron. It was a rare pleasure to be able to enjoy a leisurely lunch. Unlike the hurried American way, the Koreans seemed to savor each bite and relish deep conversations. It was apparent that many Koreans had grown up knowing that war could break out at any moment. They had learned to take their time and appreciate each day without knowing what the future held. It was an admirable trait that I promised myself to work on.

Returning to operations, I carefully reviewed the Link Control manual before contacting the Link ground personnel. Upon dialing, a female voice answered, "Link. Tech Sergeant Willis speaking."

"Hi, this is Lt. Colonel Preston calling from operations. I have a quick question for you, if you have time?"

"Sure, go ahead," she fired back.

"During my preflight walk around this morning, I noticed that the DownLink Control light was illuminated in the cockpit. Do you have any insight into how that light might have been activated?" I inquired.

After a brief pause, she responded, "No, it can only be activated from the cockpit. We cannot do that from here."

"That was my understanding as well," I affirmed. "Can you explain exactly what happens when the DownLink Control button is pushed in the cockpit?"

"Once the pilot activates the DownLink Control, our only option is to transmit new navigation points to the cockpit. However, the pilot still needs to approve them before the nav points can be loaded automatically into the inertial navigation system," she explained.

Flipping through the manual, I mentioned, "The book says the same, but during my walk around, I noticed that the autopilot was also engaged when the DownLink Control light was on. Does that strike you as strange?"

"Indeed, we have no authority over the autopilot, only the capability to send navigation data points to the plane," she responded.

Without any solutions, I found myself back at square one. I said, "Okay, I'll keep looking into it. I've requested Lockheed run some diagnostic tests after the aircraft lands to see if they discover anything on their end. Thank you for your assistance."

"No problem. Feel free to call us if you have more questions," she replied before ending the call.

"Any luck?" Terry inquired.

Shaking my head, I said, "No. This issue is bothering me. I'll be at a loss if the Lockheed tech can't find anything. It's as if I've just imagined this whole thing."

Terry reassured me, "We'll figure it out, but it might take some time."

Since I hit a dead end with the Link issue, I refocused on finishing the review of the remaining procedures. I unlocked the Intel safe and retrieved the air threats book, which remained unchanged since my last review. The North still operated older MiG-17s, 19s, and 21s, along with the more advanced MiG-23s and 29s. None threatened me at my altitude, as the -23s and -29s could only reach up to 60,000 feet, while I would be well above 70,000 feet.

Flipping through my "New Arrival Checklist," I realized that addressing the air threats was the final box to check off my list. The Air Force had a checklist for every aspect of a pilot's duties, and I was grateful for it as I got older and my memory waned. Making any simple mistake the manuals warned against, like flying over the Blue House, would result in enduring jibes from fellow pilots far into the future. Somehow, pilots always remember other people's mistakes, while forgetting about their own.

At 3:30, Brady radioed in to indicate that he was beginning his descent. I provided him with the latest weather update: hot with a slight breeze from the west, a typical summer day in South Korea.

Fifteen minutes before landing, Terry opted to join me in the car. We drove to the end of runway 27 and waited for Brady to come into view. True to form, he emerged on the final approach five minutes before landing, eight miles out.

Crossing the threshold, Brady was right on speed and at 10 feet. I maneuvered the car behind his left wing and began making altitude calls, "six feet, four feet, three feet, three feet, two feet, two feet," before the Dragon lost its will to fly and landed on both bicycle wheels at 1,000 feet down the runway. The aircraft finally came to a stop just before the taxiway. With no airflow to keep the wings level, the left wing slowly tilted to the ground until the titanium skid on its wingtip contacted the runway. The skids protected the wings in case a pilot had to slam a wing down to maintain directional control of the aircraft. There was never any damage to the wings, but the skids could chew up a concrete runway in the blink of an eye, traveling at a high rate of speed.

I swung the car around to the front of the plane and parked it so I could watch the recovery crew at work. The Dragon had been airborne for a long time and had traveled many miles.

Following at a distance, the maintenance crew pulled up on the aircraft's left side while two airmen each grabbed a pogo and headed to the lower wing. One airman used his back to lift up the wing, and the other slid the pogo into its socket and attached the pin. Then, they repeated the same process on the other wing. When they were clear of the aircraft, I gave the thumbs up to Brady so he could taxi back to the hangar.

As we approached the hangars, the crew chief took over and guided Brady with hand signals the last 100 feet. After the chocks were placed under the main wheels and external power was connected, Brady shut down the engine upon the crew chief's signal. I could see Brady was exhausted as I made my way up to the cockpit. Once Brady unlatched the canopy, I gently let it swing to its full open position. Then, I congratulated him on a successful mission. Flying for that long in a space suit is incredibly draining. Even astronauts rarely spent that much time in a space suit. I gathered up Brady's mission boards once Life Support installed all the safety pins. Then Life Support went to work unhooking Brady from the multitude of connections to the seat. As soon as he was free, Brady descended the stairs to greet us all.

It was a tradition in the Black Cat Squadron for all the pilots to gather and greet the mission pilot once they landed. There was an unspoken expectation that all pilots should be present, and if they couldn't, they needed to have a valid reason.

With the congratulations over, I turned to Brady and asked, "Any issues?"

Brady shook his head and replied, "None; she's a good jet."

I smiled and nodded, "Okay, let's put her to bed. I'll see you in debrief."

As I headed back into operations, a man approached me. "Sir, Tom Romero from Lockheed, how are you doing?" he said.

"Great, how about you?" I replied, shaking his hand. Mr. Romero was all Italian, dressed in a fine Italian shirt and dress pants. Even though Mr. Romero's appearance was remarkably better than the other Lockheed rep, he was overweight and sported a half chewed, unlit cigar out of the corner of his mouth.

"Fine," he responded. "Mr. Ross from the morning shift

informed me about what happened with the DownLink Control light this morning and wanted me to run some diagnostics. As soon as the plane is in the hangar, I will get started, if that is okay with you?"

Nodding my head, I said, "That works for me. How long do you think it'll take?"

"It shouldn't take more than an hour," he responded.

"Great. Let me know if anything comes up. I'll be in operations," I replied.

"Will do," he said as he returned to his office to gather his equipment.

In ops, I handed over the flight boards to the mission planner so that he could log all the information and secure any classified data. Then, I grabbed a cold Coke from the fridge and casually walked into Grover's office. He was engrossed in his work on the computer, but I couldn't help noticing that his inbox had significantly grown since the morning.

Contemplating how much to involve the boss in my issues, I decided to go with a condensed version. "I'm off to debrief," I informed him. "The sortie went smoothly, with no issues so far. I've asked the Lockheed rep to run some diagnostic tests on the software. Earlier today, during the plane's walk around, the DownLink Control light and the autopilot came on, so we're checking for any potential issues."

Grover stopped typing and asked, "That's odd. I've never heard of the aircraft doing that before. Did somebody accidentally activate the light in the cockpit?"

"That was my first thought, too, but I was the only one

around. I called Link earlier today, and they said there was nothing on their end. So I'm just going to have the Lockheed guy run some tests to see if he finds any Gremlins in the system," I replied.

"And Brady didn't see anything in flight?" Grover inquired.

"Nope, but I will verify again at debrief. He didn't mention anything after landing," I replied and headed out the door.

After finishing my Coke and throwing the can in the trash, I made my way to the second story of the hangar. As I opened the door to the conference room, the maintenance personnel, including the crew chief, were already in their familiar seats.

A couple of minutes later, Brady came rambling in with wet hair and took his place at the end of the conference table as the operating pilot. The head of maintenance, who ran the debrief, was seated in the middle of the table. The rest of us took up the other seats.

After getting the go-ahead from Brady, the maintenance guy meticulously read off every system on the plane to ensure everything operated normally. Even though Brady had previously confirmed everything was fine, it was standard procedure to go through a debrief to help pilots recall any details they may have overlooked or forgotten about during the flight. Once Brady indicated that there were no issues with any of the systems, the debrief was concluded. Since I had no new information about the DownLink Control light, I decided to wait for a response from the Lockheed technician before saying anything.

When I returned to operations, I peeked into Grover's

office, but he had already left for the day. I felt relieved for him, as I knew overseas operations could be extremely demanding. Long, 11-hour workdays every day of the week could take a toll on a person. It was understandable that people needed time off to recharge, especially considering that operating pilots were required to take a couple of days off after flying a high-altitude flight.

Brady and Terry headed off to the dormitory with plans to dine at a local Korean restaurant for dinner. After sorting through my emails, I let them know I'd meet them there.

Nearly an hour after landing, Tom Romero from Lockheed entered the room and reported that he couldn't detect any issues with the DownLink Control or the autopilot. After discussing the problem for the next ten minutes, we concluded that the DownLink Control light and the autopilot being on simultaneously could occur only during flight or in the test mode on the ground, which could be activated only with someone in the cockpit. I found myself shaking my head again. Some days, I hated this job. Feeling frustrated, I decided to attribute it to some unforeseen quirk in the airplane systems and move on.

I sent Grover an email with the testing results. Unfortunately, I was at a dead end with the issue, and I let him know. With that task completed, I closed up shop and left work at 5:30 in the afternoon.

Later that evening, I rendezvoused with the other pilots at a beloved off-base restaurant of the Black Cats. It had been a long day. I was worried about eating a second Korean meal for the day and the toll it might take on my body. Opting for the less spicy Beef Bulgogi, I enjoyed the thinly sliced marinated beef strips served with bib lettuce for wrapping and an array of radish, bean sprouts, cabbage, and cucumbers. All the flavors harmonized together when combined in the wrap – if I could fit it in my mouth!

We engaged in lighthearted conversation for a while before heading back to base to get some rest and get ready for the next day. Our routine was simple: wash, rinse, repeat.

As I lay in bed that night, I felt my stomach churning. It was as if my body were seeking revenge, and it was evident my stomach was not happy with me. After about an hour, the discomfort subsided as my digestive system completed its cleansing process. I eventually managed to drift off to sleep, deciding to forgo setting my alarm clock.

CHAPTER 2

The Flight

I woke up naturally the next day around ten o'clock. Terry's launch wasn't scheduled until noon, so I saw no need to get up earlier. I took a swift shower, and then headed to the dining facility for pancakes before making my way to operations.

As the last traces of morning fog dissipated, I observed the second U-2 aircraft poised on the concrete pad prepared for takeoff. Engaging in operational missions seemed almost identical to the one before, with subtle variations in takeoff times and weather conditions being the only discernible changes. Nevertheless, I still found solace in the beauty of the entire process. Everyone executed their tasks meticulously, contributing to the seamless flow of the daily operations.

Terry was preparing for his upcoming mission, reviewing any final instructions before getting into his suit. Today, he was paired with Dave Hu, who would serve as his mobile pilot.

Dave was born and lived his early years in South Korea and later moved to the United States when he was eight. Growing up in Dallas alongside his twin brother, the two developed a deep passion for airplanes, given that their home was directly under the flight path to Love Field.

Dave's grandmother, who resided with them, ensured he was proficient in his native Korean language. Although English was Dave's primary language and spoke it flawlessly, he did have the ability to communicate in Korean. His gift proved to be an unexpected advantage, especially when negotiating deals with vendors downtown. It was quite a sight to watch Dave in action. He had a unique talent for switching back and forth from English to Korean while bartering, leaving the vendor at a loss for words. He could effortlessly haggle down the price of a custom-made tailored suit jacket, pants, and shirt from $150 to just $40, leaving both seller and fellow pilots in awe of his skills.

I acknowledged both men with a friendly greeting before settling down at my desk. I wanted to ensure that there were no pressing matters requiring my immediate attention before the launch. On this particular day, I decided to take on the role of a casual observer, entrusting my line pilots to handle any potential issues that might arise. If they required my assistance, I was only a radio call away. I had learned a valuable lesson during my time in leadership school - it was crucial not to micromanage the younger pilots, as doing so would only create division.

As I sifted through my emails, I was relieved that nothing demanded urgent attention. Mr. Romero had composed his diagnostic report from the previous day, and sent a copy to Lockheed headquarters in California and included me in the email. The contents of his report mirrored what he had communicated to me the previous night. All computer systems had tested normal, and he could not replicate the problem I had encountered. I wondered that perhaps it was just another elusive issue caused by a technical glitch.

Not having any pressing tasks, I noticed the mission planner immersed in creating the paperwork for my upcoming flight the next day. I made a mental note not to rush the planner and decided to review my paperwork after lunch.

At 11:35, I quietly grabbed a portable radio and a set of keys from another mobile car and exited the door. The intense midday humidity and heat immediately caused my sunglasses to fog up as I stepped outside. To clear my vision, I instinctively tilted my head down so I could peer over the top of the glasses until the temperature and humidity equalized.

Life Support carefully secured Terry into the cockpit and disconnected his portable ventilation system. In the past, U-2 pilots faced inadequate airflow to keep them cool while taxiing, especially when the aircraft was equipped with the old Pratt & Whitney engine. The cooling system would only kick in once the Dragon Lady was airborne. As a result, on hot days the temperature inside the cockpit could quickly soar past 100 degrees, making it incredibly uncomfortable for the pilot. Beads of salty sweat would trickle down his face, stinging his eyes. Due to the sealed faceshield, there was no way to wipe it away. The only remedy was to blow air upward from your mouth to clear away the sweat. However, introduction of the newer General Electric engine resolved the cooling issue, returning the cockpit temperature to a comfortable level soon after engine start.

Captain Dave Hu stepped out of his car and ensured everything was properly connected before closing the canopy. The time was 11:45, precisely on schedule. Given the importance of the Dragon Lady mission, the control tower had instructed all other aircraft to delay their takeoffs or landings to ensure our departure was on time.

As Terry taxied onto the runway with Dave in tow, I hung back and parked my car on the taxiway. Terry gradually applied full power, and the Dragon swiftly gained speed, lifting off in less than 1600 feet. At around 80 knots, the wings flexed, and the two pogos disengaged and tumbled down the runway. The maintenance crew swiftly raced to retrieve each 75-pound wheel. There was no lingering fog today, as the midday sun had already dissipated it. I kept my eyes fixed on the plane until it vanished into the bright sky, knowing that Terry would connect into the track and begin his long day at work.

We held off on lunch until Terry made his ops normal call. Dave and I were craving some American comfort food, as a human body can only handle so much Korean cuisine. Now and then, the irresistible urge for a classic American burger would hit us, and nothing quite hit the spot like a Burger King Whopper with crispy fries and a creamy chocolate shake. As luck would have it, there was a brand-new Burger King right on base.

Upon returning from lunch, I sat down to go through my mission paperwork. My first task was to fill out the "Boldface" sheet. This one-page document had to be completed before every operational mission. The form listed eight emergency procedures. The pilot had to write down from memory all the numerous steps that made up each of those eight emergencies. These critical emergencies could arise so rapidly during a flight that a pilot did not have time to refer to the checklist and had to accomplish the steps by memory.

I meticulously reviewed my flight plan and all the relevant frequencies before taking note of all potential emergency airfields in case returning to Osan was impossible. Flying in Korea had its advantages due to its smaller size. With the exception of the far eastern part of the orbit over the Sea of Japan, I could easily glide back to Osan if I had an engine problem. In cases where the entire Korean peninsula was engulfed by fog, a pilot would have to divert to Japan to find an alternate landing field.

I completed all of my mission paperwork for my flight as the clock struck five o'clock. There wasn't much for me to do until the recovery at 9 pm. Knowing I wouldn't return to my dorm room until after dark, I decided to treat myself to a Cobb salad at the Officers' Club. The break from unhealthy spicy food was a welcome change. I decided to pick up a Club Sandwich for Dave as he chose to stay at the squadron.

As the golden sun slowly dipped below the horizon, Dave updated Terry on the weather conditions during his descent and then set off to position his car at the end of the runway. I decided to stay out of their way and parked my vehicle near the base of the tower to get a front-row seat for the landing. At precisely nine o'clock, Terry smoothly touched down.

The landing and subsequent debriefing were without incident. After a long and tiring day, I was eager to hit the sack. It would be my turn tomorrow, with a 4 p.m.

departure and a 1 a.m. landing, a grueling late takeoff time that occurred only about once every other month.

At the stroke of ten, I departed from operations and returned to the dorm. As I ascended the stairs, I passed the other pilots heading to Terry's room to enjoy a cold beer.

"Hey, boss, we're about to watch a Jurassic Park movie, you want to join us?" Terry asked seriously while Dave and Brady chuckled mischievously in the background.

The joke was on me, as Brady extracted his revenge for the newspaper incident. True to form, it didn't take long for him to reveal the details of my dream from the previous morning. "I'll pass," I replied, trying to stifle a laugh. "I wouldn't want to risk having nightmares and leave you guys to fly my mission tomorrow." I was ready for a good night of nothing but pleasant dreams.

I rose from my bed close to noon the following day. It was the most restful sleep I had had since arriving in South Korea, and I felt rejuvenated, as if my internal clock had finally been reset. Before stepping into the shower, I settled at my laptop at my desk to compose an email to my wife detailing my experiences in Korea so far. Despite having only spent six days here, I was ready for my two weeks to be over and to return home.

Turning the TV on, the worsening relations between South and North Korea dominated the headlines. The annual joint military exercises that the U.S. and South Korea had held back in March were still a point of contention, constantly provoking anger from the North Koreans and leading to threats of ending discussions with the South. However, as the year waned all would be forgiven and the two sides would eventually reconcile and resume talks. The relationship between the two countries was a predictable cycle.

Reflecting on what was possibly my last operational mission, I realized that it was bittersweet. This trip to Korea would be my last deployment before I retired. I would miss the people and the cuisine, but not the brutally long flights along the border.

After a quick shower, I prepared for Brady's arrival to pick me up at 2 p.m., hoping that any past jokes had been forgiven and forgotten.

We both agreed to grab breakfast at the chow hall even though it was well into the afternoon. For me, steak and eggs had been a staple before embarking on my flights for numerous years. As a U-2 pilot, part of our training involved learning to understand our bodies and to identify the foods that would sustain us during prolonged flights. Perhaps some superstitions were at play, but why deviate from something consistently proven effective? Besides, I loved to eat steaks.

The cook behind the counter regarded me with a neutral expression before inquiring, "How would you like your steak cooked?" Brady emitted a muffled sound and averted his eyes, barely containing his laughter.

Responding with a smile, I said to the young Air Force cook, "Medium-rare, please." I silently hoped the cook could finally get my order right this time. At the register, Brady took charge and paid for our meals, a playful payback for a jest I had made just two days prior.

While I was cutting into my steak, Brady inquired, "So, how did it turn out?"

Grinning, I replied, "You tell me."

With laughter, Brady confirmed, "Well done once again, just as you requested."

It seemed that it just wasn't meant to be.

As we drove to the squadron, I caught sight of the Dragon Lady waiting for me. Exiting the car, I paused to take in the scene. I had an incredible job, and I felt truly fortunate to have it. I knew that one day, when I looked back on these moments, I would do so with immense pride, having flown where very few had ever ventured.

Interrupting my contemplation, Brady remarked, "She isn't going to move herself."

"Roger," I replied. "We're pretty darn lucky, aren't we?"

In agreement, Brady nodded and said, "Yes, we are. There's no other job I'd rather be doing."

At the squadron, I consciously decided not to check my emails. I wanted to keep my mind free of any distractions. The mission at hand was more important than anything in my inbox. After checking in with the mission planner and finding no changes, I double checked the weather forecast. The following morning, fog wasn't expected to roll in until after my landing, and rain wasn't forecasted for the rest of the week. Instructing Brady to arrange the drinks on the right and food on the left, I headed out the door.

Upon entering the Life Support room, I was immediately struck by the sight of my meticulously arranged suit, positioned elegantly in front of a small brown chair. The first item on our checklist when arriving in the country was to drop off the suit boxes to Life Support.

The memory of my journey to Korea flooded back to me—the commercial flight, lugging two enormous white suit boxes, each weighing over a hundred pounds. I was glad the government was paying for the excessive luggage bill as it would have taken a dent out of my wallet. Inside the colossal boxes were two suits, two outer parachute harnesses, and a helmet, a pair of boots, and my trusty white long johns and socks.

Before donning my space suit, I was required to undergo a quick physical examination to ensure I was fit to fly. The assessment involved checking my pulse, blood pressure, and oxygen levels. I often wondered if my blood pressure was ever over the limit, and if so, whether Life Support would stop me from flying. As far as I knew, every pilot's blood pressure was elevated prior to taking off. Still, the Life Support personnel never said a thing to me or anyone else that I was aware of.

After my physical, I carefully removed my flight suit and donned my pure white long johns. I strolled out of the dressing room and plopped myself on the brown chair. I made a quick glance at my watch to ensure I had at least one hour before launch. A U-2 pilot needs to breathe 100% oxygen for at least one hour before takeoff to eliminate the majority of the nitrogen from the body. This meticulous process was essential for preventing the bends in the event of a loss of cabin pressurization. The bends occurred when too much nitrogen remained in the bloodstream causing extreme pain in a pilot's joints. Scuba divers similarly would experience this painful condition if resurfacing too fast.

Two Life Support technicians were standing by my side to assist me in the suit up process, while a supervisor closely oversaw the entire procedure. I carefully inserted each leg into its designated slot before ducking my head into the opening in the back of the suit. With my head and shoulders inside the suit, I stood up guiding my cranium through the neck ring. It felt like I was being born. The technicians zipped up the inner and outer zippers that ran from the middle of my back down to my crotch.

Next, I stepped into the parachute harness as the technicians lifted it over my shoulders. The harness would connect me to the parachute and the seat kit. The harness featured sturdy webbing wrapped around each leg in the groin area to help distribute the weight in case of a parachute deployment. Additionally, the harness contained a life preserver positioned around my torso. A small air canister inside the harness was designed to inflate the life preserver automatically upon contact with water. If the canister failed, I could manually inflate the life preserver through a small rubber hose.

Once the technicians securely zipped up the parachute harness, they put on my boots and attached the metal spurs. The spurs on each boot would connect to a ball on the end of a cable attached to the ejection seat. If ejection became necessary, the cables would retract, securing my feet and legs to the seat to prevent any flailing injuries.

I gently positioned the helmet over my head, ensuring the rubber seal was snug against my face. Once that was completed, each technician slid a glove onto my hands and securely snapped them into place. Fully suited up, I was guided to a comfortable brown recliner, where the technicians began to conduct leak tests on my suit.

Once the tests were completed, I was given about 20 minutes to relax. This was the time I cherished the most while in the space suit. The rhythmic sound of my breathing had a soothing effect on me. These precious moments allowed me time to reflect before the intense stress of wrestling with the Dragon would begin.

In the midst of my peaceful moment, Brady woke me up to inform me that there were no issues and that the plane was ready to go. I thanked him as he left.

As I stood up to exit the building, I could see a sign above the door that read, "Toward the Unknown." It was tradition for each pilot to tap the sign for good luck. Passing through the door, the intensity of the afternoon sun made me instinctively reach for my sun visor to shield my eyes. Despite the sweltering 90-degree temperature, my space suit kept me comfortably cool, thanks to the portable oxygen cooler carried by the technician walking behind me. This ingenious device supplied 100% oxygen to my face shield and directed cool air to ventilate the suit.

Ahead of me, the Dragon Lady came into full view. Wisps of evaporating oxygen billowed from beneath its fuselage, dissipating rapidly in the afternoon heat. Heat also radiated off the top of the plane's wings, indicating the Dragon needed to go airborne to cool off.

The clinking sounds from my boot spurs echoed across the tarmac with each step I took approaching the plane, only a short 30-yard walk from Life Support. The crew chief and two assistants stood on my left, expressing their pride of presenting me their aircraft with the traditional thumbs-up gesture. I was merely entrusted with the Dragon Lady for the next nine hours; beyond that, it was their airplane.

Inside the cockpit, a Life Support technician sprang into action. Leaning over, he secured my spurs to the seat cables, and then snapped the parachute release locks onto the harness. The young man skillfully fastened the seat kit straps and connected them to the harness before switching the oxygen hoses from the portable vent cooler to the aircraft's oxygen supply. Finally, he ensured my safety with a tight snug on my waist belt, securing me firmly into the seat.

Once strapped in the cockpit, I began my preflight checks as the Life Support technician stood by awaiting my instructions to pull the safety pins. Since Brady had already preflighted the cockpit, I quickly glanced at all my gauges, ensuring they were all in the correct positions. I opened up my checklist to the engine start page.

With everything in order, I gestured to the Life Support person to remove the five safety pins from my seat. The young man carefully pulled the primary ejection pin, followed by the secondary ejection pin, the scramble handle pin, and two pins linked to the parachute's explosive discharge. After verifying that all five pins were removed, I signaled my approval with a thumbs-up, and the technician departed with the portable cooler. With Life Support clear, Brady strolled up and performed his final check and gave me the go-ahead before closing the canopy.

Two maintenance personnel carefully removed the stairs away from the plane, as the crew chief plugged into the plane's intercom system. After a successful communication check, I informed the crew chief that I was ready for air. Within seconds, I could hear a rush of air filling the lungs of the Dragon Lady as her fan blades behind me began to rotate. As the engine reached starting rpm, I brought the Dragon to life. The rumble of the engine reverberated through the aircraft, signaling its awakening. She was ready to go to work.

After transferring all electrical power to the aircraft, I signaled to the crew chief to disconnect the electrical and that he was cleared off the intercom. The crew chief acknowledged my request and efficiently completed his tasks before walking alongside the aircraft, giving me a reassuring thumbs-up. Completing the remaining checklist items, I was ready to taxi.

Brady swiftly drove the car around and inspected the front of the aircraft to ensure the taxiway was clear of debris and all vehicles were out of the way. As he pulled off to the side, Brady's voice came over the radio, "Mobile's up. All clear." That was the signal I was waiting for.

As I requested to taxi, I received clearance to proceed directly to runway 27. Gently, I increased the throttle, prompting the heavy plane's wheels to start rolling. The crew chief was off to my right side performing his customary salute as I taxied out of the ramp area. The Dragon Lady was operating close to her maximum weight at 40,000 pounds, with half of that weight consisting of fuel. Taxiing the aircraft required complete attention to detail. With the airplane's narrow six-degree turn radius, carefully pre-planning each turn was crucial. A misjudgment could result in hitting a taxi light, or even worse, careening off into the dirt. Such an error would undoubtedly be quite embarrassing and require maintenance assistance to get the plane back on the taxiway.

As I steadily approached the runway, I felt adrenaline

pumping through my veins. The air traffic control tower cleared me for takeoff as I carefully positioned the Dragon Lady in the center of the runway. The ground crew removed the safety pins from the pogo wheels, and Brady carefully inspected the runway for any debris. After his inspection, Brady approached my left side and gave me a final thumbs-up. I responded with a confident salute. It was showtime, I reminded myself.

With a clear runway ahead, I applied the brakes and smoothly increased the power to 80%. I diligently checked all the instrument gauges to ensure they were functioning within their operating ranges and then I slammed the throttle forward to its limit while simultaneously releasing the brakes.

The Dragon Lady came to life, speeding down the runway as I kept her wings level with the control yoke. I sensed her eagerness to take flight as I approached 80 knots. At 1600 feet down the runway, with all systems operating seamlessly, I eased back on the control yoke. The aircraft smoothly rotated to a 35-degree angle, directly into the western sun. The vertical velocity indicator was pegged, indicating a climb rate in excess of 20,000 feet per minute. She ascended like a rocket, displaying the full power of the Dragon. The high-powered cold air rushed through the suit vent system, offering instant relief from the warm afternoon temperatures.

As I initiated a left-hand turn to connect into the track, the spectacular outline of the western shore of South Korea came into full view on my right side. The vast expanse of the Yellow Sea, nestled between Korea and China, was breathtaking. Departure control promptly granted me permission to climb above 60,000 feet.

Everything was smooth as the Dragon Lady was purring on all cylinders. I rolled the aircraft out to a heading of 070 to align myself with my first navigation point.

In just fifteen minutes, I was passing through 52,000 feet. I engaged the "Nav" button and the "Mach Hold" on the autopilot, giving complete control to the Dragon Lady. The autopilot would stay on till I began my descent back through 52,000 feet.

Upon reaching 60,000 feet, I activated the camera and electronic switches. The Dragon Lady swiftly began transmitting all her information to the Link personnel on the ground. With the most challenging part of my flight complete, my job now was to remain vigilant and monitor that all the systems were operating normally.

Having arrived at the first navigation point, the aircraft seamlessly lined up on its preprogrammed track, guided by the autopilot. The following navigation points were listed below the active one on the computer, ready for their turn in sequence.

As the aircraft soared through 70,000 feet, the eastern part of South Korea and the expansive Sea of Japan came into clear view. The entire peninsula, spanning just 200 miles in width, was breathtaking from this altitude.

As I gazed with the sun at my back, the "Terminator" gradually appeared in my view. The "Terminator," as referred to by U-2 pilots, marked the border between the sky and the edges of space where one could see the curvature of the earth. The fringes of our atmosphere resembled the inky blackness of night, even amid daylight hours. It was a desolate and chilling realm near the vastness of space. Peering downwards, the outside temperature gauge indicated a bone-chilling minus 68 degrees Celsius — a temperature so extreme that survival without a space suit would be impossible.

The sole discernible sound at altitude was that of my breathing. In high-altitude flight, any unexpected noise would signal an issue with the aircraft. Even the 400 pounds of thrust generated by the engine at this altitude remained soundless within the confines of my helmet. It was a serene experience piloting the aircraft where the only repetitive sounds came from its operator. Despite the constant rhythm of my breathing, the effect was so soothing that I could lose myself, oblivious to the passage of time.

My first hour of the flight was spent reacquainting myself with the stunning sights of the peninsula. From my vantage point in the sky, the entire landscape looked like a meticulously crafted miniature model complete with cities and farming communities. As the plane banked over the Sea of Japan, sunlight danced on the surface of the brilliant blue water below. Although I strained to catch a glimpse of Japan, the island nation remained too distant to see.

Completing the turn, the sun was now directly in front of me, temporarily providing more light than my sun visor could handle. I quickly reached for one of my map boards and took out a pencil to mark the time of my current position. Then, I placed the sturdy board on the dashboard to help shield the cockpit from the sun's intense rays.

During the next hour, I scanned the area from the south to the north, looking over both countries. As I gazed out, I noticed an absence of significant villages or roads in North Korea. Most of the population resided farther north, closer to the capital of Pyongyang. Despite my best efforts to discover something noteworthy beyond the DMZ, everything north of the border had stayed the same since my last flight, two years earlier.

South Korea bustled with vibrant major cities, with Seoul alone containing nearly 10 million citizens just 30 miles from the North Korean border. The potential impact of war loomed large, with differing philosophies sometimes driving a wedge between the U.S. and South Korea military. The U.S. sought to position military assets away from the DMZ as a precaution against a surprise attack with the high possibility of being overrun. South Korea, on the other hand, aimed to fortify the border to halt enemy advancement toward Seoul.

As I completed my first hour, I reached for my tube food stored in the compartment on the left side of the cockpit. I carefully selected an applesauce. Taking a hold of the hard white probe, I twisted the two together and placed the tube into the tiny slot in my helmet. I gently squeezed and a smooth blend of apples with a hint of brown sugar emerged. Peaches were next on the menu, followed by a bottle of refreshing orange juice to wash it all down.

I found myself occupied by watching the clock, gazing out the window, and daydreaming about being somewhere else. Spectators attending airshows always admired the pilots, not realizing the countless hours of monotony they endured in long missions. Most combat aircraft had uneventful take-offs and landings, while those were our exciting times. During the middle of the mission, boredom set in for us, while fighter aircraft had the thrill of engaging in bombing or shooting activities.

After circling the track two more times, I needed a bathroom break. The orange juice was refreshing, but it also meant I'd have to endure the next fifty miles relieving myself. Inflating the suit, I opened up the Urinary Collection Device valve. With the air flowing through the urine tube, I cautiously went number one. The process consisted of a lot of starts and immediately stopping to prevent backing up the system. If a backup occurred, there was a real possibility you would end up with a boot full of urine.

As the late evening approached, I finished the last of my tube foods, which provided me with the much-needed sugar boost for the remaining hours. Heading west, I observed the sun's orange glow gradually descending to meet the horizon. The beautiful sunset resembled a postcard, only to vanish a few moments later as darkness descended upon the peninsula.

As I no longer needed my map boards to block the sun, I carefully stowed them back into my flight kit. I stumbled upon a loose magazine in my flight kit that had escaped my notice earlier. To my surprise, it was filled with images of morbidly obese Japanese sumo wrestlers. The magazine was a detailed biography of the top sumo wrestlers in Japan, written entirely in Japanese. Amidst the wrestlers' pictures, several cutouts of thick steaks were taped with a caption that read, "Note. Cannot order medium-rare in South Korea." Another caption, from the rock band U2 read, "I still haven't found what I'm looking for." It was clear that the magazine was a light-hearted attempt to bring some amusement to my long flight. I made a mental note to create something even more entertaining for Brady's subsequent flight so as not to disappoint him.

As I made the turn back to the east, the moon began to rise above the dark horizon. Only half of the moon was illuminated, casting a faint reflection across the landscape. I decided to lower the lighting in the cockpit, creating a dim atmosphere and swiftly glanced over my gauges. Flying at night requires heightened awareness, as staring at an object for too long could cause it to appear to move, leading to confusion.

With the moon a quarter of the way up in the eastern sky, I shifted my gaze to North Korea, hoping to catch a glimpse of any faint lights. But to my disappointment, the expanse below seemed like a profound, lifeless void. Despite knowing the presence of people and a significant military presence near the DMZ, the area appeared eerily empty from my vantage point, which extended horizontally to 150 miles.

In stark contrast, South Korea sparkled like a magnificent Christmas tree at night. Lights illuminated the landscape from every corner of the southern peninsula, creating a breathtaking sight. The disparity between the two Koreas was glaring, resembling two distinct worlds separated by only a line in the sand.

As the clock struck midnight, a wave of weariness washed over me. Although I cherished flying, these demanding missions always took their toll on my body. Fortunately, I was only scheduled for this one flight during my two-week stint in Korea. At this moment, I was grateful I didn't have another flight before heading back to the States.

As the plane completed its second to last turn, I glanced at the track times on my flight boards before tidying up the cockpit in preparation for the final turn on the eastern part of the track for a swift descent back to base.

CHAPTER 3

The Ejection

I was tired and the plane couldn't go fast enough on the last straightaway. Suddenly, the "Master Caution" light came on and the control yoke jiggled back and forth. I scanned the multitude of indicator lights below to find out which individual system had set off the Master Caution. The "DownLink Control" light was also on. That was odd. It was the same issue I had witnessed two days earlier on Brady's flight, and I hadn't selected it. I keyed up the intercom and asked, "Link, do you have control of the aircraft?"

"Negative," Link replied.

Something was amiss. Keying the microphone again, I responded, "I have a DownLink Control light on up here."

There was a long pause before Link replied, "We do not show that we have control from here."

This was a puzzle. Just then, my two large display screens with my attitude and track map went blank. What the heck was happening? "Link, I just lost both my primary displays."

"Copy. We just lost our tracking and camera feeds. We still have all the electronic signal feeds, though."

I quickly glanced to the right side of the cockpit to make sure the camera switch was still in the on position; it was. My thoughts were racing as I tried to connect the dots between the two issues. The aircraft seemed to believe I had transferred control to the ground, but I couldn't understand why my displays went blank and why Link lost their camera feed. None of it was adding up.

In moments of confusion in the cockpit, I reminded myself it was crucial to resist the urge to randomly press buttons, potentially exacerbating the situation. My priority was not the camera but my display screens. I took hold of my checklist and rapidly flipped through the pages until I reached the section titled "Display Screen Malfunctions." Following the instructions, I first checked to see if the autopilot was still engaged, which it was. The next step directed me to recycle the display screen power switches, but despite my efforts, the screens did not reappear. Even after meticulously following all the steps in the checklist, the display screens remained non-functional.

Gathering my thoughts, I leaned back in my seat and drew a deep breath. Thankfully, the autopilot and engine were still operational. Glancing down at the Flight Management System near my left knee, I discovered a disheartening sight - my last three navigation data points had vanished except for the active one at the top of the page. Turning my attention to the backup attitude indicator, I was alarmed to see that the gauge indicated a 10-degree left bank turn, contrary to my expectation of straight and level flight. Consulting the backup heading indicator, I was horrified to find it showing a heading of 045, a far cry from the expected 080 degrees. I had crossed the DMZ and was now in North Korea.

In a moment of realization, it dawned on me that the aircraft had been in a gradual left turn throughout the couple of minutes I spent going through my display screen checklist. The subtle movement of the control yoke had eluded my attention, resulting in a small unnoticeable left turn.

I found myself in a critical situation and had to act fast. I quickly switched off the "Nav" mode on the autopilot and selected "Heading" mode. As I reached for the heading knob on the autopilot control, I realized that I had no displays. Without any visual indicators, I couldn't locate the heading bug. Frustrated with myself, I muttered a reminder to think before pressing buttons. With my right hand, I reached down and grabbed the manual turn knob on the autopilot control panel.

Amidst the chaos, and before I could turn the aircraft, the operator on the Link communication system urgently announced, "Dragon 02, we are detecting a missile launch of two SA-2s."

Looking at my defense gauge, I noticed two targets on the outer ring at my 2 o'clock position. A buzzing sound in my headset confirmed the imminent threat described by the Link operator. It was clear that the missiles had been launched from an SA-2 site near the DMZ coastal area.

I found myself facing a crucial decision as I tried to make my way back to South Korea. A turn to my right was the quickest route, but that would take me straight into the path of oncoming missiles. I knew my jammers could potentially handle the missiles, but I was not confident enough to risk my life on that one measure alone. Instead, I decided to turn left away from the missiles, but this would take me deeper into North Korea.

"Link, what's the best heading to get out of the threat ring?" I yelled.

"Dragon 02, we are still unable to track your location to give you that information," they responded.

"Copy," I replied, realizing I had forgotten they had lost their tracking system. With no location information, I calculated that the missiles were approximately 24 miles away from me. I remembered from my threat briefing two days earlier that the SA-2 had a 27-mile threat range. With my aircraft traveling seven miles per minute, I knew I needed more than three miles to reach a safe zone. However, at my current heading of 010 and turning left, I also knew I would need to fly at least a 330 heading to achieve maximum separation between me and the missiles. As my heading approached 350 degrees, every second became critical in my race against time.

I focused on the standby heading indicator until it showed 330 degrees. Glancing at the clock, I pressed the timer button, silently urging the aircraft to go faster. As I rocked back and forth in my seat, I wondered how I had ended up in this nerve-wracking situation and what the heck had happened to my display screens.

The missiles would take a minute to reach my altitude, and I calculated they were launched 15 seconds ago, I had 45 seconds left. It would take me 25 seconds to travel the three miles I needed to hit the maximum missile range.

With this information I had about 20 extra seconds to spare to improve my chances.

I refocused on the defensive gauge, watching the targets close in on my position until they were almost inside the inner ring. All I could do now was wait, trusting that the jammer systems were working to confuse the radar signals and giving me a fighting chance to escape the incoming threats. The Dragon was testing my patience today, but I was determined to beat the monster.

Dear Lord, please get me out of this situation, I kept repeating. I was sucking down oxygen like there was no tomorrow as my faceplate started to fog up around the edges, even though it was heated. Ten seconds to go. Five seconds. Zero seconds. The only sound I could hear was my heaving breathing. I told myself I would give it an additional 15 seconds before celebrating to be sure I had not miscalculated the numbers. I could not imagine the destruction a 35-foot-long missile flying up my tailpipe would do. It would be over immediately.

As the additional 15 seconds passed, I maneuvered the aircraft into a maximum left-hand turn, heading back south. I couldn't be certain whether my electronic countermeasures had disrupted the missiles' guidance systems or if I had put enough distance between us to evade them. Nonetheless, I felt a glimmer of luck on my side, which I desperately needed at this moment. "Link, I'm initiating a turn to the south," I yelled through the intercom, banking the aircraft up to 20 degrees.

"Link, this is Dragon 02. We've detected multiple SA-5 missile launches but cannot pinpoint your exact location."

In that intense moment, it crossed my mind, "Here we go again." I quickly checked my defense systems, but my screen showed no signs of any missiles. Suddenly, a white streak from above the aircraft struck the plane's left wing. The impact caused the plane to jolt further to the left, but miraculously, it kept flying.

Immediately, the autopilot disengaged light came on. I gripped the yoke tightly, feeling the aircraft pulling even farther to the left; I slammed the yoke to the right to get back to level flight. Despite my efforts to counteract the turn, the damage to the left wing from the missile made it almost impossible to return to straight and level flight.

The realization hit me that the situation was dire. The Dragon Lady was no longer airworthy, and I had to say goodbye. However, doing so while the aircraft was still in a turn could prove fatal. I needed to stabilize the plane for a few crucial seconds to ensure a safe ejection. With my left hand steering the control yoke to the right, I threw the autopilot switch on and reengaged it, desperately hoping it would hold. Thankfully, it did. I cranked the turn knob as far right as it would go. I released the control yoke and prayed that the autopilot would counteract the left-hand turn. It did.

I could feel the powerful vibrations from the autopilot's clutches as it was desperately fighting the aircraft. It was a futile effort. The autopilot would only be able to hold for a few more seconds. That was all I needed, I told myself. I quickly reached down with urgency and grasped the bright yellow ejection ring handle between my legs. With every ounce of strength, I pulled the ejection ring.

The left and right canopy thrusters exploded, propelling the canopy away from the aircraft. Simultaneously, another explosion below my seat followed. As I was being propelled up the steel ejection rails, the last thing I saw was the autopilot disengagement light coming on and the aircrafts bank angle at 45 degrees and increasing.

The sheer force of the ejection was unlike anything I had ever experienced. The intense compression on my spine and the overwhelming forces made it challenging to stay conscious as my vision began to blur.

Clear of the aircraft, the ejection seat stabilization rockets roared to life. The ejection system's gyros were swiftly correcting my angled ejection from the aircraft to an upright position. It felt like an eternity before I could open my eyes, but all I could perceive was utter darkness. There was no sense of space or direction, just an overwhelming blackness. I could only hope that one of the aircraft wings would not swing around and swat me out of the air, instantly killing me.

Then, I realized my sun visor had slipped down during the ejection, intensifying the darkness. Struggling against disorientation, I lifted my hand and pushed the visor up on my helmet. Repositioning my helmet's visor revealed a faint horizon illuminated by the moon's pale light. Off in the distance, lights twinkled dimly. It had to be South Korea, as I knew there were no lights to the north of the DMZ. Yet, the southern lights appeared farther than I expected. It dawned on me–then—I was deep behind enemy lines.

I reminded myself to focus on the present moment and avoid dwelling on what had gone wrong or how to find my way home. I was still in a precarious situation. As the seat plummeted toward the earth, I could feel the rush of air against my body. I relied on the small 6-foot drogue chute, a miniature parachute attached to the top of the ejection seat to keep me stabilized. I could sense that it was functioning correctly. Without it, I would have been tumbling out of control. Thankfully, the ejection system had performed as expected so far.

Despite my heightened heartbeat and body temperature, the freezing cold air was seeping through my space suit. The temperature at my altitude was hovering around minus 68 degrees Celsius, a stark contrast to the 26 degrees at ground level – a staggering 94-degree difference.

My mind then turned to seat separation. The seat was meant to thrust me clear at 15,000 feet above sea level, allowing ample time for the parachute to deploy. However, how could one gauge 15,000 feet in the darkness? I pondered the possibility of distant lights giving me some perception of height. If I could discern the outlines of objects on the ground, it meant that seat separation had failed, leaving me hurtling toward the ground, trapped in the ejection seat.

I needed to ensure I had a backup plan, so I carefully reached for the scramble handle on the ejection seat's right edge. Even though I couldn't see it, I could feel the distinct outline of the yellow and black striped handle. Pulling this handle would release me from the seat and deploy my parachute, providing a manual way to detach from the ejection seat if necessary.

I tried to occupy my mind by thinking about my descent to keep myself focused on the present. I estimated that I was descending at approximately 90 miles per hour and calculated that it would take approximately nine minutes to reach the ground from the ejection altitude. However,

I needed to subtract the 15,000 feet, which equated to around two minutes. Judging by the time elapsed since the ejection, I estimated I had about five minutes left in the seat. It was just a waiting game now.

Suddenly, five minutes later, and with no warning, I was forcefully separated from the seat. A loud, unexpected bang near my left ear startled me as the parachute shotgun shell charge exploded, contributing to the opening of the 35-foot chute above me. Most military parachutes were only 28 feet, but mine was larger due to the added weight of the space suit and seat kit, totaling an extra 70 pounds.

The sudden jolt caused by the parachute opening left me gasping for air. The jolt was much more intense than I had anticipated. The force pressed hard against my body, especially around my crotch. The parachute harness was designed to absorb the full impact of the opening shock and I could feel the strain on my legs.

As I looked straight down for the first time since ejecting, I was met with a pitch-black area, devoid of distinguishable landmarks. The parachute gently swayed in the night sky, creating an unsettling stillness. I had no sense of the wind's direction or my direction of travel. I decided to hold off on using the nylon six-cord risers until I knew which way I needed to go. Pulling the six-cord risers would allow excess air to escape from the back of the parachute, giving me some control over my direction. Clearly, I wouldn't be able to drift all the way back to South Korea on the parachute alone.

I carefully attempted to free myself from the frayed spur cables dangling from my boots. Thank goodness the retraction cables worked flawlessly, and I could sense both my legs were still attached to my body. The frayed edges of these cables posed a grave danger of puncturing a life raft if I landed in the water. Since I couldn't see below me due to my helmet, I had to rely on instinct to remove the remaining cables. By using the toe of one boot against the heel of the other, I managed to dislodge the cables and free them from my boots. One ejection step completed, I reminded myself.

As I floated through the air, a sense of fear gripped me as I realized that my parachute beacon could be broadcasting my location to both U.S. forces and the enemy. The last thing I wanted was to end up in a North Korean prison. With determination, I traced the left riser with my fingers until I found the small black plunger attached to the webbing. Gripping it tightly, I pulled it downward, hoping to shut off the beacon and avoid detection. I had no way of knowing if my efforts were successful, but at least I was able to complete another checklist item.

Peering below, I strained for any sense of height above the ground. Taking a glimpse of the horizon, I could see distant lights, indicating that I was still up relatively high. I desperately searched for any recognizable landmarks but found nothing. Worried about forgetting other crucial tasks, I berated myself for not deactivating the beacon during my ejection. As I turned my helmet from left to right, I strained to spot any signs of an explosion caused by my aircraft, but everything remained eerily dark.

Waiting a few more minutes, I searched again for my landing area. Surprisingly, there were no trees in sight below me. It was quite puzzling, considering that the southern part of North Korea was typically covered in trees. I couldn't believe my luck – had I come across the only clear patch of land suitable for a parachute landing?

As I got closer, I realized that the area below wasn't clear; instead, it reflected light. I immediately realized I was directly above a lake. If I didn't take corrective action, I would end up right in the middle of it. Landing in a lake and dealing with the associated challenges was the last thing I wanted to face. I recalled the story of a U-2 pilot who had ejected and landed in the Sea of Japan years earlier. He hadn't been able to make it into his life raft and tragically lost his life. I was determined not to meet the same fate, as my survival depended highly on the parachute landing.

Instantly, a bright light caught my attention from the corner of my face shield. The explosion appeared about three miles to my right, and I knew it had to be my aircraft. Fortunately, the distance between myself and the wreckage gave me some breathing room. Now my goal was to put the lake between me and the wreckage, giving me precious time to evade capture. If my ejection seat landed in the middle of the lake and sank, it would also delay the North Koreans in determining if I had survived or died in the wreckage. Eventually, I knew they would search the wreckage for answers, but that would take time. If the enemy had picked up my beacon, they wouldn't even bother searching the wreckage for me.

Floating in the sky, with both hands, I reached up and pulled the six-cord risers. Instantly, I could feel the rush of air from the back of the chute, propelling me forward. Glancing down, I realized I was still positioned directly over the sprawling lake and heading south. If I continued in this direction, I would indeed land in the expansive body of water that stretched before me. The closest shoreline was to my left, and I urgently needed to adjust my course to reach solid ground. Determined, I reached up with both hands, grasped the front left riser, and exerted all my strength to pull it down. At first, it was difficult to discern if the parachute was responding, so I repeated the process, exerting even more force, until I could sense the canopy gradually veering to the left.

As the ground was rapidly approaching, I continued tugging on the left riser, altering my trajectory to align directly with the narrow shoreline. However, the daunting prospect of landing in the densely forested area beyond the shoreline made me apprehensive. What if I overshot the landing zone? What if I became entangled in the trees, unable to free myself? My parachute draped over trees would make it easy for the enemy to locate me. Also, the thought of crashing into a tree and sustaining multiple injuries was another alarming possibility. I was facing an impossible predicament with no favorable outcome. With that in mind, I was determined to try to land in shallow water.

As I drew nearer to the shoreline, the moon's faint glow revealed the separation of water and forest. Beyond the dense forest, darkness made it impossible to discern any open space in which to land. I made some minor adjustments to my parachute. Still, as I descended, I realized I wouldn't reach the narrow shoreline. Instead, I was heading 25 yards deep into the thick, unforgiving trees.

With no way to fix my overcorrection, now I braced myself for a potentially rough landing amid the trees. I decided against releasing the seat kit, fearing it would only complicate matters by inflating the raft and making things even more challenging. Instead, I hoped the kit would offer some protection for my rear end as I prepared for impact.

Closing in on the trees, I crossed my arms over my chest, protecting myself from any protruding limbs that could cause harm—the moment of impact happened in waves. First, I felt a sharp blow to my left shin as I collided with a large limb, and then I broke through some smaller limbs on my way to the ground. Somehow, I had managed to avoid a direct hit on the larger branches. The sudden impact of hitting the ground caused me to roll several times along the forest floor before coming to a stop on my back.

I lay still for what seemed an eternity before finally mustering the courage to open my eyes. As I carefully assessed the situation, I focused on detecting any potential pain or discomfort in my body. To my relief, I didn't sense any immediate effects from the rough landing. Gaining some optimism, I began to test my limbs, verifying that my initial assessment was indeed correct. My breathing was rapid and intense as my body processed the shock of the entire event.

Satisfied that I hadn't sustained any significant injuries, I reached up and unlocked the visor of my helmet to allow for better airflow. The humid, sweltering air felt suffocating yet invigorating against my face. I was alive.

It was then that I noticed my right foot suspended in the air. The parachute cords had somehow become entwined around my leg while the parachute remained tangled in the nearby tree. It became evident that when I had rolled over upon landing, the cords had ensnared my leg.

Despite my sincere efforts, I struggled to free myself from the stubborn parachute cords.

Recalling the small knife tucked in a sleeve pocket next to my left thigh, I removed my gloves, unbuttoned the pocket, and retrieved the knife, secured by a nylon cord. Depressing the button on the side of the vibrant orange grip enabled a four-inch blade to pop out. I carefully maneuvered the knife and began cutting through the tangled cords. It took considerable effort and time, but eventually, I freed myself from the parachute. I took a deep breath and was feeling optimistic about my situation. It was a miracle I had not killed myself, and so far, had no broken bones that I could detect.

After managing to stand up, I felt the full weight of exhaustion hit me. My body was operating solely on adrenaline at this point. I realized that I urgently needed to discard the pressure suit. Navigating through a dense forest in a heavy, thirty-five-pound pressure suit during the heat of late July was a recipe for disaster. The same suit that had kept me insulated and alive in the unforgiving, freezing altitude now posed a threat of overheating with potential heatstroke.

I disconnected my helmet and tossed it on the ground. Then, I released the parachute from my harness, clicked off both seat kit attachments, and let the kit drop to the ground. With the seat kit out of the way, I unzipped the front of the parachute harness, slid it down my legs, and stepped out of it. I then sat on the ground, unzipped my boots, and carefully placed them aside.

Next, I began the process of unzipping the space suit. Getting out of the suit required some contortion, as I had to wiggle my way out of the back of the suit. Doing this solo was quite a challenge. Usually, after a regular landing, I would have had the assistance of two Life Support technicians to help me out of the suit.

I cut a two to three-foot piece of parachute cord to aid me in unzipping the space suit. I tied it around the small opening in the metal flap on the outside zipper located near my crotch. Using the cord, I pulled the zipper up from my groin area to my lower back and then I repositioned the cord over my shoulder and pulled the zipper the rest of the way to the fully open position near my back shoulder blades. I repeated this process for the inner zipper. Once both zippers were completely open, I crouched and maneuvered myself out of the suit. It was quite a struggle, but I eventually pulled my head through the opening. Finally, I was free from the suit and all its weight.

After discarding the suit, I found myself in a predicament. All I had on were my sweat-drenched white long johns—consisting of a top, bottom, and socks—which made me stand out like a sore thumb in the darkness. It puzzled me why the Air Force didn't provide us with gray or dark green long johns for operations in Korea. It was clear that they hadn't foreseen this situation, and neither had I.

My first priority was to retrieve my parachute from the trees and conceal the rest of my gear. As I tugged on the parachute cords, I was relieved to find that the chute wasn't severely tangled in the trees. The chute got snagged about 10 feet above the ground. Despite hearing some branches snap, I put all my weight into freeing the last panels by pulling on the cords, even lifting my feet off the ground for extra leverage. Unfortunately, that didn't work, so I resorted to bouncing up and down to increase the pressure. Suddenly, a loud crack pierced the stillness of the night as a large branch separated from the base of the tree, and the chute came crashing down beside me. Thankfully, I managed to sidestep a six-inch diameter branch to avoid being hit.

After bundling up the parachute into a large mass of nylon, I opened my seat kit. I retrieved the small one-man life raft and then took out the survival kit, which was stored in a thick, waterproof rubber bag with a sturdy zipper to keep its contents dry. Although the dim light made it hard to see inside, I relied on touch to identify the items. I recognized the PRC-90 portable radio and pondered sending a quick transmission to alert rescue of my survival, but I decided against it. I doubted whether a rescue team had been mobilized yet. I didn't want to risk signaling my location to the enemy. It was the same dilemma I had faced with the parachute beacon. Any attempt to establish contact would have to wait.

I recalled the contents of my lower left suit –pocket—a cell phone and some maps. I placed the survival bag down and unzipped the pocket on my space suit. Unfortunately, the old flip phone was in pieces, presumably damaged from the impact of the limb. It was disappointing, as I had hoped to inform my squadron mates of my ordeal, but reaching a cell tower in North Korea was probably unlikely. However, I did find a folded-up map of the entire peninsula, which I planned to study later to orientate my location.

Continuing with my search, I delved deeper into the survival bag. After some rummaging, I found the compass, unwound the attached string, and placed it around my neck. Satisfied I had the essentials, I zipped up the bag, planning to take more detailed inventory later. It was time to get rid of any evidence and start heading south.

Hearing the distant sound of a helicopter, I wondered if the North Koreans had already located me. Gathering my parachute, raft, helmet, space suit, and seat kit, I concealed them near two large trees. The late summer foliage provided good cover. I held still as the helicopter passed by a few hundred yards to the south, heading westbound. I guessed they were en route to the crash site.

As the humming sound of the helicopter faded away, I rose to my feet with a surge of determination. Surveying the array of gear at my feet, I pondered the best course of action for disposing of it. The thought of concealing such a significant amount of gear without a shovel left me with only two options: hide the articles in the dense forest or sink them in the lake with the help of some rocks. However, the prospect of being exposed in the open lake while submerging the gear made this option seem unfeasible, especially with the risk of helicopters patrolling the area.

I took a few moments to meticulously scan the surroundings, searching for a suitable spot to stash everything. I knew this decision could potentially buy me precious time to make my way back across the border. While my initial instinct urged me to abandon the gear and start running, I realized that if the authorities found my gear, they would know that I was alive and on this side of the lake. It was imperative to ensure that I concealed everything as effectively as possible to maximize my chances of escape.

After careful consideration, I discovered three decaying

logs nestled against several trees, creating ample space to conceal all my gear. Methodically, I transported each item to the makeshift hiding place and took one final glance at the pile to confirm that I hadn't overlooked anything critical. The realization that I couldn't risk returning to retrieve anything forced me to ensure I had everything necessary before continuing my difficult journey.

I carefully tucked the seat kit, parachute harness, and my helmet underneath the logs, ensuring they were well hidden. As I prepared to stow the space suit, I deliberated whether to take the gold outer cover. Eventually, I decided I needed it for added protection and to help cover my white long johns.

The gold space suit cover, although just a thin outer layer, served to conceal the unattractive interior of the main space suit, which resembled a balloon encased in a fishnet to prevent bursting. I carefully unzipped all the connection points to the cover, and when freed, I put it on my body. The cover was designed for the suit and was significantly larger than my frame. I resolved this issue by cutting a 20-foot nylon cord into smaller segments. I then tied it around my waist, thighs, and ankles to secure the cover, ensuring it wouldn't snag on any branches as I moved through the forest. Although the cover was too light in color, it was still an improvement over the high visibility of my white long johns. I would have to address darkening up the gold cover at a later time. Now was the time to move.

After stowing the parachute and the rest of the space suit, I prepared to depart, taking only my boots and survival kit. To conceal any trace of my gear, I used my knife to cut small branches and strategically placed them to cover any signs of my belongings. Stepping back, I was satisfied to see that in the darkness, nothing was visible.

I sat down next to a tree as I put my oversized boots back on. With ease, I slid my arms through the weathered straps of the survival kit, slinging it over my shoulder. Taking a moment to secure the kit and ensure it was comfortably positioned, I surveyed the surrounding area one last time. Had I forgotten anything? Satisfied with my preparations, I set off back toward the lake.

My goal was to approach the lake as slowly as possible, aware of the potential risks of encountering inhabitants near the shore. I knew it would be best to stay near water as I would need more water than what my survival kit contained. The harsh heat demanded a constant supply of water to stay hydrated.

Unlike lakefront properties in the States, there were no visible structures in this remote North Korean lake. Slowly making my way closer to the shoreline, I noticed the calm water, its gentle waves creating a soothing, rhythmic sound.

Grabbing my compass from around my neck, I unfolded the sturdy metal ends, attempting to discern the heading. Despite my best efforts, the darkness made it nearly impossible to read. Taking a knee, I carefully placed the compass on the ground and activated the light on my watch. Disappointed to find that the watch light was also insufficient, I paused momentarily. Then, I recalled the small white penlight stowed in the left shoulder pocket of the gold cover. To my relief, it was right where it should be, undamaged from the ejection and protected in its sleeve. Shining the light on the compass, the direction along the shoreline showed 185 degrees. With my bearings now established, I felt confident in moving forward.

I plunged back into the dense forest, cautiously traveling parallel to the shoreline. After covering just 200 yards, it became clear that this journey would take much longer than I had anticipated. The zigzagging path through the woods was four times slower than walking in a straight line along the shore. and I had to move gingerly to avoid stepping on any broken branches that would shatter the silence of the night.

As I trudged on, I noticed my boots were ill-fitting and cumbersome. They were designed for the space suit and were too big, producing loud, clunky noises that disrupted the natural stillness due to their oversized design. These size 13 steel-toed boots were not intended for hiking through the forest. Weighing three pounds each, they were far from my usual size ten footwear. Going barefoot was out of the question and there were no spare shoes in my survival kit. I resolved to find an alternative, but before I could think further, the faint hum of another approaching helicopter reached my ears, this time coming from the west.

Instinctively, I sought refuge amidst a dense thicket of bushes, positioning myself in the middle of the cover. As the helicopter drew nearer, I felt a surge of confidence, knowing that I was well hidden within the foliage, unlikely to be spotted by anyone aboard the craft.

The sound of the rotating blades grew louder, prompting me to look up through the dense canopy and catch a glimpse of the twin-rotor helicopter passing directly overhead. Judging by its design, I assumed it was a Russian-built troop hauler. I was curious if it was the same helicopter that had flown over earlier. It seemed likely, as it followed the same route, but in reverse. I speculated that it was probably returning to its base.

After the helicopter disappeared from view, I gathered my strength and resumed my journey. My pace was slow, and I found myself preoccupied with the dilemma of what to do with my boots. Failing to come up with a solution, I kept moving forward.

Fatigue began to overwhelm me as time passed, hitting me like a sudden wave. All I desired was to collapse onto the ground and drift to sleep. I realized that I was reaching the point of exhaustion, and if I didn't stop to rest, I might resort to irrational decisions. Glancing at my watch, I was surprised it was already 4:10 am. I had presumed it was closer to two o'clock. Despite not having covered much ground, I knew I couldn't continue.

Scanning the surroundings, I identified a tree with low branches to climb. I removed my boots, concealed them in the shrubbery, and ascended the tree. Weak from the exertion of the day, I struggled to climb. When I reached about 10 feet high, I settled into the middle of three branches protruding outward. It was the best spot I could find, given my condition. With dawn approaching, I desperately needed rest. My mind was drained, and all I could think of was sleep.

CHAPTER 4

The Plan

The persistent buzzing sound filled the air around my head, abruptly ceasing when the kamikaze fly finally landed. Half-dazed, I instinctively fluttered my hand in the vicinity of the fly's last location, only for the buzzing to resume once more. This peculiar game of attack-and-retreat persisted for what felt like an eternity until I finally gave up and let him win.

I struggled to open my eyes and take in my surroundings. I suddenly became aware that I was perched in a tree as the previous night's events came flooding back. I attempted to swallow, but my tongue was parched and stuck to the roof of my mouth, signaling the state of dehydration that my body was in.

The harrowing encounter with the determined fly finally came to an end as it abandoned its quest and flew off in search of another target. Fully awake, the realization set in that this was not a bad dream—this was real.

I squinted at my watch, which displayed the time as two

o'clock. As I tried to readjust my position, I discovered that my left leg had fallen asleep. Using both hands, I carefully readjusted my leg to restore my circulation. The sensation of stinging needle pricks shot up and down my limb, but the renewed blood flow soon relieved the discomfort. I glanced down to ensure that my boots were still where I had left them, hoping that no creature had carried them off while I was sleeping. Thankfully, they remained right where I had placed them in the darkness.

The shimmering gold of my outer suit cover glowed brightly in the daytime, making me easily noticeable in the tree. To make matters worse, my white socks stood out like beacons without my black boots on. Before setting out tonight, I knew I had to camouflage myself to blend into the night better.

I reached for my map and spent a few moments orienting myself to the different topical colors. It was hard to differentiate the uneven terrain of North Korea. After intense scrutiny, I managed to pinpoint a sizable lake about eight miles north of the border. In all likelihood, this had to be the same lake where I found myself, as it was the only one depicted on the map.

I was 100% certain I was on the eastern part of the lake. The wider part of the lake looped to the east and then veered north. If I chose to stick close to the shoreline, I would have to travel an additional five miles to the east before resuming my journey to the south, adding a couple of days to my night-time only travel. However, a narrow section of the lake, approximately the width of two football fields, seemed to present an opportunity for a crossing in order to continue heading south to safety.

Once I swam across the lake, I would have to journey east

for a short distance, which would lead me to a good-sized valley where I could navigate south to the border. This route promised to be the easiest and safest path to take.

As I unzipped my survival kit, my heart raced with anticipation. The first item I pulled out was the yellow PRC-90 radio. I unhooked the flexible rubber antenna and attempted to turn it on, but there was no click when I turned the on/off knob. It then struck me that the radio had been packed with the power on, and now the battery was dead. Frustration filled me as I envisioned myself screaming at the Life Support supervisor. It probably didn't matter. If I tried to communicate with search and rescue, the enemy would surely pick up my signal and be here within an hour. Radio communication would probably be out of the question. I had to think of something better.

Refusing to let discouragement take over, I proceeded to unpack three Mylar water pouches. The first two I quickly drained, and ate both of the dense granola bars. Despite what little nourishment the bars provided, I knew I would have to acquire sustenance along the journey to keep my strength up. Recalling my survival training, I remembered the advice to let your stomach act as a canteen when water is scarce. With this in mind, I consumed the remaining Mylar water pouch.

Continuing to sift through the contents, I discovered a raft repair kit, which was unnecessary since I had already disposed of the raft. The next item was a silver desalination pump, which was equally useless since I had plenty of fresh water close by. However, one item inside the bag caught my eye. As I examined the assortment of flares – two day/night flares and a Gyro Jet flare – I decided to keep them in case they might be instrumental in securing a helicopter rescue. I also remembered that the Gyro Jet flare could double as a weapon. The flare could launch a tiny red bullet-like cartridge up to 700 feet in the air.

I reached deeper into the survival kit and pulled out three signaling mirrors tied together. I kept the mirrors away from the sun so I would not inadvertently send a bright signal to some North Korean aircraft flying above my position. I recalled from my training, a signal from a mirror could be seen up to 30 miles away, a vital tool for attracting attention if needed. I made a mental note to save the mirrors to use when I was closer to the border.

Next, I found a clear plastic water container and a bottle of iodine pills. The pills were essential for purifying any contaminated water I might find, ensuring it would be safe to drink. The heavy-duty plastic bag could hold roughly half a gallon of water for my hydration needs. My plan was to fill up the water bag before heading out tonight.

As I sorted through the remaining items in the survival kit, I found a pair of white socks, a small first aid kit, miniature binoculars, and some matches. The idea struck me that an extra pair of socks could offer more protection if I had to remove my boots. While it wouldn't fully safeguard against sharp objects, it could provide an added layer for my tender feet.

Suddenly, a crazy idea came to me. If I cut some of the leather from my oversized boots and placed it in between my two pairs of socks, which might provide a makeshift sole. The improvised design could protect the bottom of my feet, making traveling a lot easier.

I hastily stuffed everything back into the survival kit before carefully descending from the tree. I knew I was taking a big risk by cutting up my boots, but I had no choice – they were slowing me down, and I needed to move faster. As I began to cut into the thick leather of the boots, the distant sound of a helicopter caught my attention. I strained to see through the dense canopy, trying to determine their direction. I waited until the whirling sound disappeared before continuing cutting the leather. The leather was tougher than I expected, and I had to be cautious not to injure myself. After a struggle, I managed to fashion a makeshift leather pad that closely resembled my foot.

I carefully retrieved the extra pair of socks from my survival kit and took the ones I was wearing off. I then maneuvered each leather pad between the socks and then slid them back on while adjusting them simultaneously. The additional layer of protection felt reassuring. Using some tape from the first aid kit, I wrapped it around my ankle and the middle of my foot, ensuring the sock would not slide off. After testing my new design with a few steps, I was pleasantly surprised by how well they worked. I felt more agile and could move more quietly than in my noisy three-pound clunky boots.

I decided to conceal what was left of my boots, raft repair kit, and saltwater pump in the bushes to lighten my load. After ensuring the items were hidden as best as I could, I nestled myself in some thick bushes, hoping to catch at least a few hours of rest before nightfall.

At first, every little sound in the forest seemed amplified. I attempted to mimic an owl, moving my head only in slow motion in the direction of the noises. It was a waste of time, as they were simply natural forest sounds. If I inquired what every sound was, I wouldn't get any sleep, and fatigue was a bigger threat to my health than the sounds of nature. It struck me how fortunate I was to parachute into a forest instead of landing in a city where escape would have been impossible. I recalled the fate of Senator John McCain, who had been captured immediately after ejecting into downtown Hanoi during the Vietnam War, and I considered myself lucky to at least have a chance to evade. However, I knew the extent of that chance remained uncertain.

Over the past six days, I had diligently worked to adjust my sleep schedule from U.S. time to Korean. Now, I was faced with the challenge of once again resetting my body clock for sleeping during the day and staying awake at night.

Exhaustion finally overcame me, and I drifted off into a state of semi- consciousness. I would awaken ever so often just enough to check for darkness. The relentless presence of flies and the stifling humidity made it difficult to rest for any length of time. I couldn't risk falling into a deep slumber and potentially sleeping through the night when I was supposed to be traveling.

Eventually, the sun dipped below the western horizon, casting the forest into darkness. I made myself wait a full hour after sunset before venturing out. As my eyes adjusted to the night sky, I cautiously made my way down to the water's edge, attuned to every sound in the forest. First, I needed to replenish my water supply, then locate a mud hole, and do my best to dull the bright colors of my outer garment and socks.

As I neared the shore of the lake, I hesitated, scanning

the area for any signs of human presence or approaching aircraft. Satisfied that the coast was clear, I waded into the water. The gentle lapping of the waves soothed my nerves.

Wading up to my knees, I carefully filled my container as full as it would go and zip-locked the top. Eager to minimize my exposure, I swiftly made my way back to the shelter of the forest, uncertainty gnawing at the back of my mind about how long it would take for the iodine pills to purify the water. Not wanting to wait too long, I shook the bag, forcing the pills to dissolve quickly. Relieved that the water seemed untainted, I cautiously took a sip, filtering it through my teeth to catch any impurities. To my surprise, the odorless liquid was clean.

I eagerly waited for an additional ten minutes, curious to see if I would experience any reaction from my first sip. Sensing no adverse effects, I proceeded to consume half of the contents within the container. Carefully resealing the bag, I stuffed it back into the survival kit. It dawned on me that I would have to find water before daybreak; otherwise, I would be forced to endure the day's scorching heat with very little to drink.

I set out on my next task, determined to find some mud. I located a spot near the lake that jutted close to the tree line and reached down to grab a handful of the slimy stuff next to the water's edge. The gooey mud had a pungent smell of dead fish, quite unpleasant compared to the odorless water I had just consumed. I proceeded to coat my socks and outer garment with the black mud. Continuing to rub handfuls of wet earth all over myself, I made sure to cover the front side of my body completely. To cover my backside, I had no choice but to lie down and swish back and forth. Once satisfied that there were no bright colors showing, I smeared some mud on my forehead and around my neck. Despite the awful smell, the gooey stuff offered some relief from the muggy night's heat and the biting insects.

Eager to continue my journey, I checked the time on my watch using my pen light, which read 10:55 pm. I followed the same strategy as the night before, staying about 25 yards into the woods to avoid encountering people or wildlife near the water's edge. However, I soon faced steeper hills than the previous night, making it challenging to parallel the lake. The inlets forced me to zigzag east and then back west to stay along the coastline, consuming precious time. It was my only option; otherwise, leaving the coastline, I might lose my bearings.

I quickened my pace through the dense woods with my senses on high alert for any unusual sounds. After a couple of hours, I decided to take a break and hydrate. Despite eating the granola bars, the only food supplies in my survival kit, I could still feel the gnawing emptiness in my stomach. I would have to find food sooner or later.

With no food, I had only water to fill that emptiness in my stomach. Finishing the remaining water in my container, I decided to fill it up again. Adding the iodine pills to the plastic bag, I approached the water's edge. Not wanting to redo my socks with mud again, I took them off. Venturing into the water, I bent down to fill my bag.

Close by, I heard a low grunting sound from my left that startled me. I strained my eyes to see through the darkness, but the moonlight was too dim to reveal the source of the noise. I held my breath, listening intently as the grunting drew nearer.

My thoughts raced as I scanned along the shoreline in hopes of identifying the sound. It didn't sound human, but beyond that, I had no idea what it was. Slowly, I began wading into deeper water, hoping that if it were an animal, I would stand a better chance in the water than on land.

With each step, the water rose higher up my waist as the unsettling grunting sound grew louder, drawing nearer to me. Scared out of my wits, I was shivering, even in the warm water. Suddenly, a blurry figure emerged at the water's edge, catching my eye. As our gazes locked, a silent standoff ensued. It was a tense moment, a game of chicken. Then, surprisingly, the creature rose onto its hind legs, revealing itself to be a bear.

Fear permeated every part of my body. Could this bear swim? Weighing my options, I waded farther into the water, now up to my chest. I could only hope that the bear wouldn't dare pursue me this far into the water.

The bear, however, seemed undeterred, sniffing the air. My heart was racing, waiting for the bear to make its next move. I had only one option and that was to swim away from the shoreline.

I felt for my switchblade in its protective pocket. It was no match, but it might deter the bear if I got a lucky jab. The moonlight revealed the bear's features when standing - a distinct light-colored patch on its belly. Probably an Asian bear, I thought to myself. I was now in a standoff, a game of chess, waiting for the bear to do something.

Finally, the bear made his move. Hunching over, he snatched one of my socks, vigorously shaking it. I silently pleaded for him not to take it. As he continued to shake the sock, he must have sensed something inside. It had to be the leather pad and the bear was determined to extract it.

In a desperate attempt to distract the bear and recover my sock, I emitted a low growl, but it had little effect. I couldn't risk making too much noise and drawing even more attention to my predicament.

After failing to dislodge the leather, the bear gave up and began to wander off, sniffing the area as he went. While I was relieved that the bear was leaving, I soon realized that he was headed in the same direction I needed to go. Once I was confident that the bear was a safe distance away, I carefully made my way out of the water.

On dry land, I slid my socks back on, cringing as I felt the dampness of the bear's saliva next to my skin. It was a revolting sensation, but I was grateful to still have both socks intact as I retaped them.

Needing a moment to collect myself, I settled at the edge of the forest and retrieved my map. With the help of my penlight, I estimated that I had covered about a mile, with another mile ahead of me, before I reached the point where I would have to cross the lake. Holding my penlight in my right hand, I couldn't ignore the trembling that still coursed through my arms. Encountering a bear face-to-face was a first. What other creatures did North Korea have in store for me?

The lake meandered along, leading me first to the west and then looping back to the east. I paused at intervals to quench my thirst with a few sips of water, but my hunger pangs persisted. I was aware that people could endure weeks without nourishment, but I doubted they were expending all their energy traveling through the night like I was.

Remaining alert to my surroundings, I halted periodically to listen for any signs of life ahead. I resumed my journey only after I was satisfied that it was safe.

Making my way eastward, I followed the coastline as it transitioned into a sheer cliff. I had no other choice but to ascend the rugged hills above the water. I had taken the time to replenish my water supply, knowing that navigating down the cliffs to get water was not ideal.

Pausing for a brief rest, I checked my watch and saw that it was 3:30 am. I realized that I needed to keep moving if I wanted to cross the lake before daybreak.

An hour later, I reached the peak of the final hill. Walking to the cliff's edge, I peered down and saw that I was approximately 50 feet above the water's edge, with waves crashing against the wall. The map hadn't indicated the presence of such a formidable obstacle. If I continued along the north side of the lake, the distance from the opposite side increased, making it much farther to swim across.

On the bright side, I confirmed my location on the map and was able to spot the opposite shoreline. My estimations seemed accurate as the landmass on the other side of the lake seemed to be approximately the distance of two football fields away from where I stood. I was confident in my ability to make the crossing. Despite not being an experienced swimmer, I was certain that I could paddle backward while holding onto my survival kit.

Surveying my surroundings from the cliff, I noticed a strip of shoreline to my left, around 500 yards from my position. The moonlight reflected off the metal roofs of several structures near the water. This was the first sign of human habitation I had seen since my ejection. However, I couldn't take the risk of trying to find a path down to the village, as any local dogs might alert the residents.

The only choice I had was to descend the cliff below me. Jagged plates of rocks jutted out from the sandstone surface, offering precarious footholds for my descent. The steep incline made sliding down impossible, and I couldn't risk leaping into the unknown depth of the water below. A fall from this height would mean checkmate for me.

As I pondered my predicament, I scolded myself for not packing more parachute cords. Shaking off the thought, I focused on my problem at hand.

Glancing at my watch, I saw that it was 4:45 a.m. I realized that I would have to halt my journey for the time being and find a way down or an alternative route. The idea of retracing my steps for half a mile back to where the cliffs started was discouraging. The quickest option seemed to be to scale down the cliff here and swim across the lake.

As I paced back and forth on the forest floor, devising a plan, my eyes caught sight of thick, winding vines coiled around the trunks of several trees. In a moment of inspiration, I contemplated whether these vines could be my key to maneuvering down the treacherous cliff face. I envisioned tying several vines together like a makeshift rope, providing me the means to descend.

With determination, I set out to put my plan to the test.

Taking hold of the thickest vine I spotted, I cautiously shifted my weight onto it, hanging suspended beside the tree. However, my optimistic anticipation quickly turned to dread as a sharp, thunderous crack shattered the tranquility of the forest. Dead tree branches crashed down around me, entangled with the vine, causing a chaotic deluge of debris. I sought refuge against the tree's sturdy trunk to shield myself from the jagged limbs. Twice now I was spared by crashing limbs.

Moments passed, marked by the stillness in the forest. Assured no one had heard my escapade, I gathered the vine and returned to the cliff's edge.

Tossing the vine over the edge, I strained to discern whether it reached the water below. In the dim moonlight, I struggled to gauge the distance accurately, but figured I was short.

Retreating into the woods, I located a slightly thinner vine. Mindful of my previous mishap, I opted not to place my weight on it. Instead, I ascended the tree as far as I dared, with plans on using my knife to sever the vine.

Cautiously perched on the tree at a considerable height, I commenced the arduous task of cutting through the resilient vine. Despite the challenge, I persisted, switching to the serrated edge on the opposite side of my knife to facilitate the process. After an intense struggle, I triumphed as the vine finally yielded to the blade.

Tying the two pieces of the vines together, I made my way back to the edge of the cliff and tossed the vine over. I swayed the vine back and forth, hoping it would reach the water below. The darkness still made it difficult to gauge, so I hauled the vine back up and felt for moisture. Success! The vine was wet, indicating that it reached all the way down. I was relieved to have solved this problem and headed back to the shelter of the trees. As the first glimmer of light appeared on the eastern horizon, I crouched behind some fallen logs, feeling a mix of triumph for getting this far and disappointment for not making it across the lake before sunrise.

I drifted in and out of a daze, briefly roused by the distant sound of passing helicopters. I awoke feeling utterly drained, my body heavy with exhaustion. Finishing the rest of my water supply, I forced myself to remain still and burn no more energy than needed. Relentless flies pestered me in my weakened state. Deprived of the strength to fend them off, I resigned myself to their onslaught, hoping they would get their fill of blood and depart. Despite smearing dirt on my face, the persistent creatures found ways into the crevasses.

As dusk approached, I forced myself to remain alert, listening for any sounds. The thought of the bear frequented my mind. Perched atop the hill, I watched the sun sink below the horizon, casting a tranquil glow over the landscape. Unperturbed by my presence, a deer ambled by, oblivious to my concealed position amid the foliage. After an hour of darkness, I mustered up the strength to rise. The gnawing hunger in my stomach had subsided, but I felt some of my energy had returned through the daytime hours. I reminded myself once across the border I could eat and sleep to my heart's content. I had to keep pressing on.

Before descending the cliff, I took a few moments to stretch my legs, avoiding the threat of cramps. Gathering the two vines, I made my way to the cliff's edge, where I identified a robust tree capable of bearing my weight. I secured the vine around the tree with a bow tie knot. Then, I set about testing the strength of the vine. Anchoring my feet next to the base of the tree, I pulled with all my might to tighten the knot as snug as I could get it. Feeling sure the vine would not slip, I tossed the remainder over the cliff.

I carefully made my way back to the logs and retrieved my survival kit. After removing my socks, I stowed them in the kit. Making sure the bag was fully inflated, I securely zipped it up. Hopefully, the trapped air would provide some buoyancy and assist me in the water.

With the survival kit strapped to my back, I grasped the vine with both hands. Holding on tightly, I began to lower myself down along the rocky surface. Each step was a challenge as I searched for secure footholds, testing each one before putting my full weight on it. I knew that if the vine were to break, I would have to attempt a water landing by pushing off the ledge with my feet. Ten feet down the cliff face, the vine was holding.

Suddenly, I was startled by the unexpected flutter of two birds that flew out from their nest on my left. I momentarily lost my footing but managed to maintain my grip on the vine. The surprise almost caused me to plummet into the water below. I struggled to find another secure foothold, eventually finding a stable rock for my right foot. As I stood there, taking deep breaths, the only sounds in the air were the beating of my heart and the faint tweeting of baby birds calling for their parents.

As I looked down, I noticed that the vine seemed to be short of reaching the water. How could this be? I had measured the length perfectly. Then it dawned on me – I had forgotten to account for the part of the vine that was wrapped around the tree trunk. I could only hope that it wasn't too short.

I gripped the vine tightly, feeling the rough texture against my palms as I descended hand over hand. With each movement, I made sure to secure my footing. As I reached the end of the vine, I peered down and realized that I was close to eight feet above the water's surface. Holding on to the end of the vine, I took a deep breath and hoped that the water below was deep enough. Without hesitation, I let go and plummeted into the water, slicing through the surface like a dart. I was relieved as I did not touch the bottom underwater. As I resurfaced, I clung onto a protruding rock, catching my breath.

I focused on taking large, controlled breaths before embarking on swimming across the lake. I adjusted the straps of my survival kit, holding the kit against my chest, making sure the zipper was on the bottom to keep the trapped air at the top resembling a flotation device. Feeling prepared, I pushed off from the cliff edge using my legs to paddle and propel myself across the lake. I made a conscious effort to minimize any noise from my movements by keeping my feet below the water's surface.

As I continued paddling, I periodically checked my course, ensuring that I was on track to reach the land on the opposite side of the lake. To maintain my direction, I spotted the tree I had previously used to tie the vine to. By using the tree as a guide, I was able to paddle in a straight line.

A sense of apprehension washed over me as I paddled 100 feet away from the vertical cliff. I knew this swim was going to be more challenging than I had initially anticipated. I focused on regulating my breathing to provide the maximum amount of oxygen. I was also struggling to maintain a straight path, realizing that my right leg, being my dominant one, was causing me to veer slightly to the left.

By the time I reached the 200-foot mark, I had settled into a steady rhythm. I relied solely on the strength of my legs to propel me forward. As my temperature rose, I could feel sweat trickling down into my eyes and mouth. Pausing, I ducked my head into the water to rinse off the salty beads on my face.

My legs began to burn with exertion as I approached the halfway point. I decided to rest and change positions. Lying in the prone position with the survival kit in front of me, I began kicking my legs gently. Although this provided temporary relief, the burning sensation soon returned.

Suddenly, I sensed a faint vibration in the air. I ceased kicking and strained to listen to the new sound. Sure enough, the distinct whirring of helicopter blades reached my ears, bouncing off the water. I realized that I was marooned right in the middle of the lake.

I couldn't believe it. I was so close that I would have reached the opposite side of the lake in another ten minutes. As I waited, straining my ears to locate the source of the approaching helicopter, the sound grew louder and more ominous. I frantically considered my options and finally decided to position the dark survival kit over my head, hoping to remain unnoticed. The chopper soon appeared over the hill to the south of my position, menacingly close. The cloudless night meant I

small mercy in the face of my despe[...]
pulled my socks out of my survival kit an[...]

Once concealed behind the trees, I switched [...] penlight and swiftly located my position on the m[...] Using my compass, I plotted a course that involved heading south along the coastline for approximately half a mile, then tracing the water's edge to reach an isthmus located between two hills. After crossing the narrow isthmus, my route required me to continue eastward, following a stream between some larger hills before crossing into a vast north-to-south valley that would guide me straight to the border.

Empowered by a renewed sense of determination, I secured the survival kit on my back and started off in a southerly direction. According to the map, my destination for the night lay three miles ahead, but considering the dense woodland, I estimated my journey to stretch closer to five miles.

My proximity to the shoreline facilitated my progress, albeit leaving me exposed in some spots. Negotiating the irregular inlets like the night before added additional time to my journey, but it was unavoidable. Periodically, I halted to listen for any auditory cues, but the silence urged me to press onward.

I arrived at the isthmus at close to 1:30 a.m., under the cover of darkness. The narrow strip of land stretching between the two hills was just 80 yards wide. I knew this passageway would likely be a thoroughfare for animals and, potentially, people.

Taking caution, I crouched low and surveyed the area for any signs of activity. The only creature in sight was a

_____ shoreline. With no time _____ ersed the narrow pass.

_____ lized I was walking amidst _____ nts – it seemed I had stumbled _____ a garden. Pausing, I knelt down _____ ings for any signs of human _____ gs. But the dark veil of night offered no c_____ by presence.

As my eye_____ ced downward, I noticed a cluster of spherical objects nestled within one of the well-tended rows. They appeared to be some variety of melons, each about the size of a cantaloupe. My stomach stirred with anticipation at the thought of substantial nourishment rather than just sips of water.

Carefully, I unzipped my survival pack, stashed two of the melons inside, and secured it shut again. The added bulk of the melons made the bag bulge at the seams as I hoisted it onto my shoulders, hastening my pace to leave the area.

As I marched along through the wilderness, a wave of excitement washed over me at the thought of finally indulging in the sweet, juicy melons. I had never felt such anticipation for a meal before. Determined to savor the experience, I decided to wait until I had settled down for the night before cutting them open.

Suddenly, the sound of a helicopter became audible, prompting me to seek cover in the denser part of the forest. I held my breath as it passed overhead, surmising that it was likely headed for a refueling stop before continuing its search.

Pausing to consult my map, I estimated that I had

approximately two miles to cover in an easterly direction before reaching my destination for the night. With this in mind, I took a moment to rehydrate, consuming half of the water in my container before resuming my journey.

Glancing at my watch, I noted the time—2:30 a.m. I cautioned myself to proceed cautiously and resist the urge to rush so I could devour the melons. Although eager to taste them, I refrained from inspecting their ripeness, knowing that I was going to eat them regardless of their state of maturity.

Advancing eastward along a nearby stream within the valley, I found the terrain more forgiving than the challenging hills I had traversed earlier. Encouraged by my progress, I set my sights on reaching my destination before daybreak.

I constantly scanned my surroundings for any signs of movement, whether from people or animals. So far, the only activity of life I saw was the raccoon. As I covered another mile, I decided to take a breather and finished the last of my water. I refilled my container from the stream after adding more pills. I found myself rotating my head from side to side to hear and see anything out of the ordinary in the wilderness around me. The forest was quiet.

Continuing alongside the stream with a mile left to cover, I anticipated the ascent up the hills and planned to navigate along the military crest, a strategy developed for downed airmen to traverse three-quarters up the side of mountain ridges to avoid potential encounters with adversaries positioned at the peaks or down in the valley below.

At 5:15 in the morning, I caught sight of the expansive valley stretching north and south. This valley would guide my way to the south and to safety. I began the gradual ascent up the ridge.

As the sun's rays gradually pierced through the ridge on the opposite side of the valley, I scoured the area, struggling to find any trees with low branches that would provide an opportunity for climbing. The lack of suitable pines and the aged hardwood trees offered no footholds for scaling.

Finally, I stumbled upon a heavy thicket of sweet-smelling bushes. Clearing away the excess small limbs, I nestled into the thickest part and arranged some cut brushes to conceal my lower extremities. Opening up my survival kit, I retrieved the two melons, the moment I had eagerly been anticipating.

Checking for ripeness, I inhaled the aroma of each melon but found no definitive scent. With my survival knife in hand, I carefully sliced around the entire perimeter of one melon, releasing a cascade of seeds from the center. After scraping out the seeds, I proceeded to cut the flesh of the melon into inch-wide chunks, relishing the small comfort it provided despite not being fully ripe. Each bite was gratifying to my body as the sun ascended over the opposing ridge. After finishing one half of the melon, I promptly started on the other half.

I carefully considered whether I should save the remaining melon but ultimately decided to devour it. After finishing both melons, I inverted all four halves to prevent flies from gathering. I draped the extra thickets over my body for added camouflage and used my survival kit as a makeshift pillow to rest my head on. As I settled down for the day, I silently commend myself for the significant distance I had covered. After the challenging swim, I had initially thought I might not be able to travel any farther for the night, but I was surprised my strength had returned, and I was able to make it to my destination before daylight. With food in my stomach, I succumbed to a deep, recovering sleep.

CHAPTER 5

The Encounter

The sudden whooshing sound jolted me awake from my deep sleep. As I lay there trying to make sense of the noise, I checked my watch and realized it was 10:30 in the morning. Another swish echoed through the morning calm, accompanied by hushed voices. This was not a typical forest sound.
Faced with a dilemma, I weighed my limited options. If I tried to run for it, whoever was out there would likely spot me. I had no choice but to stay put and hope that the source of the sound didn't come any closer.

My heart pounded in my chest, and a familiar ache resurfaced, reminding me of the adrenaline-fueled moments of my ejection. Doubt crept in as I questioned my decision to travel along the military crest.

The dense forest muted the whooshing sounds, but someone was definitely approaching my position. Suddenly, the possibility of the Army searching for me crossed my mind, but It did not correlate with the helicopter scanning the area on the other side of the lake. Had I left a trail, and had they already caught up to me?

As the sounds drew closer, I could make out a man and a woman's voices between each whooshing sound. The voices were clearly in pursuit of something. As they paused to converse and rustle through the underbrush, I took in my surroundings, and then it hit me: I was hidden amidst a vast patch of wild blueberries, intermixed with other non-desirable shrubs. It dawned on me that the voices belonged to berry pickers.

With nowhere to conceal myself, I apprehensively prepared for their imminent arrival. I retrieved my knife, knowing full well that it paled in comparison to whatever was causing the whooshing sound. Still, it was the only weapon at my immediate disposal.

I tried to calm myself while holding my breath for fear of making any sound. With one final whoosh, I was face to face with a young man and a girl.

Both were more startled than I was. The boy pointed his three-foot Machete directly at me. His hand was shaking as the blade wobbled from side to side. He asked me something in Korean, but I did not respond with words or facial expressions.

As my eyes scanned the intruders, they fell upon a young man with unkempt black hair, clad in a frayed, dark-hued tank top and weathered brown shorts. His dilapidated sandals barely clung to his feet, and he cradled an old Folgers coffee can half filled with blueberries in his left hand. Every aspect of his body bore tell-tale signs of destituteness. Off to his side stood a young girl in similarly tattered attire. It was evident that they were in dire shape.

The young man met my gaze with a scrutinizing squint, silently evaluating my presence and motives. Meanwhile, the girl sought refuge behind him, stealing glances in my direction with a timid curiosity.

From their appearance, I surmised that the man was approximately 18 and the girl a year or two younger. This led me to ponder—were they a struggling couple navigating the unforgiving wilderness in search of sustenance and survival?

The atmosphere was tense as the young Korean man stood before me, still holding his Machete and waiting for my response. I remained silent, unsure of what to do.

In a whisper, the girl accompanying him spoke into his ear. After consideration, he asked me in broken English, "You American?"

I hesitated, wondering if they were aware of my recent ejection. Choosing to stay silent, I gazed at them.

Sensing my reluctance, the girl murmured something to the man and then retreated behind him. He nodded in agreement with her, then asked, "You pilot?"

Now I was sure they knew who I was. I chose not to say anything but hold my tongue. In my mind, I surveyed my next move. If they were going to turn me in, I would have no choice but to kill them both, a thought that was horrible and unpleasant on so many levels. First, I had probably less than a slim chance of beating a Machete with my little switchblade. Second, I had a daughter about her age. Could I look my daughter in the eye for the rest of my life, knowing I took the life of a little girl like her? That would be unbearable.

The man's frustration was evident as he inquired, "You go to border?"

His question left me thoroughly puzzled. It seemed they were after something more than turning me in to the authorities. I nodded and replied quietly, "Yes."

My response triggered a flurry of rapid-fire questions from the girl. At times, it seemed like she was orchestrating the conversation, but it was evident that only he could speak English.

I sat still, observing both of them intently. They seemed lost in their thoughts, contemplating their next move. It was evident that the girl was urging the man to ask me something. Still, he appeared hesitant, perhaps because of uncertainty about his limited English or because he was in a disagreement with the girl.

Finally, the man blurted out, "We take you to border, you take us to America?"

With that response, it became clear why there had been such a prolonged exchange and hesitation. Realizing the gravity of the situation, I hesitated before agreeing to their terms. I felt I had no choice; refusal could lead to dire consequences. It was apparent that they had loftier plans in mind than just seeking a reward.

Relenting with a smile, I replied, "Yes. You help me; I will take you to America." The man conveyed my response to the girl, who attempted to conceal her joy, though it was visible in her eyes. They had nothing and were willing to take a significant risk to aid me, all in pursuit of a better life than the one they were living.

I released my grip on the knife and gestured toward the young man. "Your name?" I inquired.

The boy nodded and pointed to himself. While still holding the blueberry can, he replied, "Yu-jun. Her name Ji."

It was clear that our communication was going to be slow and challenging. Still, we were able to understand each other on a limited basis. I considered showing them my map and indicating my destination, but I hesitated. I still wasn't entirely sure if I could trust them.

Pointing to my chest, I said, "My name is Dan."

Yu-jun didn't respond; instead, he tried his best to translate to the girl.

I then asked, "Is she your wife?"

With a straight face, he translated my question, and she burst into laughter.

"No, she younger sister," he responded, as they continued conversing in Korean about what would come next. A minute later, they had reached an agreement. Yu-jun stated, "We need to go now."

As I was about to get up off the forest floor, the distant sound of more voices echoed through the trees, growing louder with each passing moment. With a gesture, Yu-jun signaled for silence, and they crouched low, waiting for clarity in our situation. They were now in the same position I was in a few minutes earlier. The boisterous conversation drew closer while we remained concealed from view inside the berry patch. The men's voices echoed off the hillside just 20 yards above us.

Yu-jun and Ji exchanged glances, their subtle smiles

hinting at an understanding that eluded me. Sensing my curiosity, Yu-jun attempted to convey the essence of what was transpiring, but without success. His reassuring gesture pleaded for patience as we waited for the men's conversation to conclude.

The voices gradually faded as the men departed. "We have to leave now," Yu-jun repeated.

Carefully disentangling myself from the branches, I retrieved my survival kit. Peering up the hill, I followed the siblings out of the berry brush. As the wind swept through the foliage, I caught the smell of human excrement, explaining Yu-jun and Ji's subtle smiles earlier.

Glancing in that same direction, I caught sight of a surface-to-air missile site adjacent to a target-tracking radar. Two formidable missiles, each 30 feet long, were positioned on a mobile launcher. The operators were the voices we heard relieving themselves. Vast camouflage netting covered the entire site. At the same time, the target tracking radar silently scanned the skies above in a vertical motion. I couldn't help but wonder if this was the site responsible for firing at me. However, it was impossible to know for sure, and ultimately, it didn't make any difference.

Yu-jun confidently led the way to the east, carefully guiding his sister down the hill, with me trailing behind. Occasionally, they would glance back to ensure I was still following. I wondered if I had made the right decision by following them, but I reminded myself there was no other choice.

As we ventured farther down the hill, I finally called out

to Yu-jun, realizing we were going in the wrong direction. I intended to stay near the military crest and head south. I quickly pulled out my map and gestured to our current location and the direction I wanted to pursue. However, it seemed Yu-jun needed help looking at the map, so I resorted to pointing at all of us and then motioning southward.

Suddenly, his eyes snapped open, and he responded, "No. Many troops with guns that way. You follow us. We go that way," as he motioned toward the east and down the hill.

I reluctantly accepted Yu-jun's familiarization with the area and felt relieved, believing he was telling the truth. I couldn't fathom a reason for him to lie after wanting to help me.

We journeyed through a dense, tangled forest, navigating twisting trails with deliberate and cautious movements. The trek in broad daylight filled me with apprehension, but again it seemed I had no other option. After traveling for 15 minutes, we reached a small stream nestled in the valley below. I considered asking my companions to halt so I could refill my water container, but I assumed that since they didn't carry water, they must have access at our destination.

We silently crossed the stream and ascended the opposite ridge, with Yu-jun continuing to lead the way.

Approaching noon, we finally reached a diminutive hut concealed deep in the woods. The structure measured no more than 15 feet by 15 feet in size. The four corners were constructed with small tree limbs, while smaller bamboo poles were intertwined vertically between the trees, held together by vines. The roof consisted of nothing more than a plastic tarp blanketed by large banana leaves.

Having previously visited Appalachia in America and witnessed poverty, I thought I was prepared for extreme poverty. However, what I saw here surpassed anything I had ever encountered before. Instead of opening the front door, Yu-jun lifted it and moved it aside, revealing the stark conditions within the hut.

At that moment, Ji entered the house and emerged with a delicate white porcelain bowl. She placed it on a small table outside and bent down to grab a wooden bucket of water to fill the bowl, gesturing for me to clean up, so I followed her instructions. As the warm water flowed over my hands and onto my face, I felt a sense of rejuvenation. It was as if the water were not only washing away the physical dirt, but the weariness from deep within my body. Even though I realized I would need more than just a simple wash to truly get clean, the basic act did refresh my spirits. Ji then handed me a torn piece of towel to dry myself.

An outdoor fireplace adorned with large rocks was near the table. Above the remnants of a previous fire, a makeshift metal bar served as a place to hang a pot for cooking.

After drying off, Yu-jun invited me inside their house. As I entered, my gaze fell upon two hammocks gently swaying, suspended from the corner posts of the humble abode.

In the middle of the room, a modest wooden table sat upon the dirt floor, the main focal point in the room. Two 5-gallon upside down plastic buckets were repurposed as makeshift seats. Placed on the table was a well-worn translation book titled "Korean to English" which I knew to be the source of Yu-jun's endearing yet imperfect English.

Due to the absence of windows, the hut relied solely on natural light streaming through gaps in the bamboo walls. Several 5-gallon plastic buckets were grouped in one corner, with one containing potatoes and another holding larger fruits similar to the ones I had enjoyed earlier. A small tarp shielded the remaining buckets. In the opposite corner, a small, weathered gray pail sat next to a stack of old newspapers, serving as an improvised indoor bathroom.

A wire stretched from one side of the hut to the other side as a makeshift clothesline, supporting an array of clothes in various drying stages. Dull silver cooking pans and assorted utensils were neatly stacked on another table along the far wall, signifying the hut's functional yet humble possessions.

Ji motioned for me to sit on one of the upside-down buckets. A makeshift cooler built into the ground was revealed as she lifted a wooden lid on the floor. She delicately reached inside and pulled out two perfectly formed round rice balls with small fish heads protruding out. Despite their limited possessions, she extended the rice ball to me with a sense of humility. I bowed in gratitude as I accepted the food, understanding the significance of her offering.

Positioning myself on one of the buckets, I accepted a small plate that Ji handed me to use. Though starving, I resisted the urge to devour the whole rice ball in one go, wanting to be considerate of their hospitality. Ji gave Yu-jun the other rice ball, and he joined me. I wondered if I was the first American they had ever seen. I was sure he was waiting patiently to inquire about my experiences in the United States.

Pulling a photo from the translation book, Yu-jun handed me an old black and white picture and said, "Mom and Dad."

The photograph captured a happier moment in their family's history, when everything seemed brighter, with smiles on their faces. Unsure of how far to delve into the delicate situation, I trusted my intuition. As I set down the rice ball and with an inquiry look said, "Where now?"

Though Ji likely didn't understand my question, her distress was visible as she sensed the direction of our conversation. After a brief pause, Yu-jun said, "The Army say Mom and Dad traitors and execute them two summers ago."

With a concerned but puzzled look, I asked, "Why?"

In response, Yu-jun retrieved a broken two-way radio and placed it on the table. With tears welling in his eyes, he explained, "Dad, try to get hold of brother in the south. The Army says owning radio grave offense, then execute both our parents."

In a gesture of solace, I draped my arm around Yu-jun's shoulder. Sensing the depth of their resentment toward the Army, I refrained from asking additional questions. It became apparent that their profound aversion to the Army was likely why they chose to protect me from soldiers.

I refocused on enjoying each grain of rice, taking small

bites, and relishing every mouthful. After finishing, Ji kindly offered me another rice ball, but I graciously declined. I didn't want to risk being too greedy, unsure if I had already eaten their only meal of the day. Ji then presented me with a small bowl of freshly picked blueberries, a gesture I warmly accepted. I marveled at their effort to gather those sweet, juicy blueberries, walking as far as they had.

I eagerly emptied the bowl by popping two berries at a time into my mouth. I turned to Yu-jun and expressed my gratitude, asking him to convey my thanks to his sister. He understood and relayed my wishes to Ji in Korean, and Ji nodded in appreciation. I sensed that Yu-jun had many questions for me but still refrained, for which I was relieved. It was 1:30 in the afternoon, and exhaustion was taking hold of my body. I was completely drained.

Recognizing my fatigue, Yu-jun offered me use of one of the hammocks, and I gratefully accepted. I removed my dirty, smelly socks, which I regretted not having done earlier, although I sensed that they were unconcerned about tracking dirt onto their floor. I settled into one of the hammocks, positioning my survival kit below me.

As I lay in the hammock, gently swaying back and forth and feeling the breeze sneaking in through the door, my eyelids grew heavy, and I fell into another deep sleep. It was the most restful slumber I had experienced since sleeping in my bed at the base.

When I awoke three hours later, I was alone in the room. The two companions I had been with were nowhere to be seen. I carefully rolled out of the hammock and checked to see if my survival kit was still there. It was. Untouched, and in the same spot I left it.

Trying to gather my thoughts, I noticed a small mirror hanging on the wall by a string. Suddenly an idea popped into my head and I needed to locate Yu-jun. Then it occurred to me that they might have left me. Maybe they'd had second thoughts.

I grabbed my survival kit and looked for the young Koreans outside. I searched the entire perimeter of the hut but couldn't find them. In a hushed voice, I took a chance and called out, "Yu-jun."

I spotted Yu-jun and Ji rising to their feet about twenty yards away. I walked in their direction, and as I approached them, I noticed two small mounds of earth with vibrant wildflowers adorning the graves. Two makeshift crosses, crafted from tied-together sticks, rose above each resting place. It was evident that Ji had been weeping.

I observed from a respectful distance, not wanting to intrude on their solemn moment at the gravesites. After they had finished, both made the sign of the cross, a clear indication of the Catholic faith. It struck me deeply that they were practicing their religion in a place where it was forbidden, marking them as outsiders. It was a moment that gave me insight into the challenges they faced.

Yu-jun stood up, and in his broken English, told me, "We say goodbye to Mom and Dad. We leaving to America."

As Ji walked back toward the hut, I sensed her need for solitary reflection. It was now evident that they had resolved to accompany me back to America and would have to leave their parents' graves behind.

Rummaging through my survival kit, I retrieved a sizable mirror. I gestured toward the sky, hoping Yu-jun might understand what I was trying to communicate. I needed an open space devoid of obstructing trees to use the signaling mirror effectively. I pointed at a nearby tree and shook my head while pointing to the sun. Yu-jun seemed perplexed and unable to comprehend my request.

I stood on the hillside holding the mirror, brainstorming my next move. Yu-jun suddenly had an idea and motioned for me to follow him. I hoisted the survival kit onto my back, and we began our ascent up the hill, pushing through dense forest. Five minutes later, we finally reached a clearing a few acres in size. Somehow, Yu-jun had finally understood what I was asking. I took a moment to survey the open area in relation to the afternoon sun.

Positioning myself in the sunlight and facing south, I held out my left arm with two fingers extended. I grasped the mirror in my right hand. With careful precision, I peered through a visual hole in the center of the mirror to catch the sun's reflection and bounce it off my outstretched fingers. Like a marksman sighting a target, I adjusted the mirror's position until I could manipulate the reflection with minor adjustments.

I carefully angled the signaling mirror to scan the southern sky. I wanted to catch the attention of any friendly airplanes patrolling along the border. After a minute of meticulously moving the mirror, I noticed the sky was clear, with no visible vapor trails from incoming or outgoing airliners flying near the DMZ. I had heard that these signaling mirrors could be effective up to 30 miles, but I was having doubts about those claims.

As ten minutes passed, my initial optimism started to wane. I wasn't exactly sure what I was expecting, but it seemed like the signaling mirror was not living up to its reputation. Just as I was about to give up, I cast one final glance at the southern sky. I was surprised to see a faint vapor trail appearing and disappearing intermittently. I quickly adjusted the mirror to focus on that part of the sky, making slight adjustments to ensure precision. The white trails reappeared, and, to my amazement, a second one appeared beside it. While I couldn't spot any aircraft, the trails were unmistakably visible.

The two military aircraft were releasing streams of fuel. I continued to wiggle the mirror, targeting the two white lines in the sky. With no signs of the aircraft, it was hard to determine what type of planes they were. Most likely they had to be fighter aircraft as they were too high to be search and rescue.

Excitedly, I pointed to the sky to show Yu-jun, but he seemed unsure of what I was pointing at. "They see me," I exclaimed.

Peering up at the sky with me, Yu-jun asked, "Who sees you?"

Filled with joy, I responded, "The Americans. Do you see the lines in the air?"

"Yes, I see," he replied.

"I'm fairly certain those are military fighter jets up there. I'm not sure if they are American or South Korean. They released fuel because they saw my signal," I proudly explained. I had completely forgotten about the signaling mirrors until seeing the mirror in the hut, which jogged my memory.

Upon finishing with the mirror, we began our journey

back to the hut. I felt a surge of hope about our prospects of rescue. Yu-jun expressed a keen interest in learning about America and my personal life there. I'd had a sense it was going to be brought up sooner or later. I shared the story about my upbringing in Texas and my childhood aspiration of becoming a pilot. However, I realized that discussing my favorite foods in a place with scarce resources might be inappropriate. I swiftly transitioned the conversation to my experiences as a farmer, reminiscing about operating tractors and the moments of pure bliss during the harvest season.

Throughout our exchange, Yu-jun was so engrossed in what I was saying that he nearly tripped a few times as we neared the hut. He yearned to hear more, but I decided to save additional stories for later.

As I lingered outside, I refilled my water container from the bucket beneath the table. After dispersing two iodine tablets into the container, I securely sealed it and stowed it back into the survival kit. A strange premonition crept over me as if this would be my final opportunity to procure water before reaching the border.

In the background, I could hear Yu-jun conversing casually with his sister before emerging from the entranceway clutching a coffee can, minus the blueberries. Grinning warmly, he beckoned, "You come with me."

I walked alongside Yu-jun, feeling content, but still worn out. I hoped for a quick nap before a potential departure later that night. The uncertainty of our departure time left me needing clarification about our schedule.

As I followed Yu-jun down a narrow trail through the

woods, we stumbled upon a breathtaking tropical area nestled under the forest canopy. The abundance of ferns in this hidden oasis was genuinely remarkable. Yu-jun dropped to his knees without hesitation and began digging with the same coffee can that had contained the blueberries earlier. The well-used coffee can was a valuable tool in their daily lives.

Intrigued by his actions, I, too, started to dig in the soft soil with my hands, unsure of what we were searching for. Moments later, Yu-jun triumphantly held up a root. His excitement was contagious, and I began to dig faster, fueled by the prospect of finally having a substantial meal. Within ten minutes, we had collected a dozen roots for cooking. With the coffee can almost full, we ventured to another area and gathered red and golden raspberries, adding vibrant colors to our foraged bounty.

Yu-jun remained vigilant, constantly scanning our surroundings for any potential threats.

"Are you looking out for people?" I asked him, but he shook his head and replied, "No, bears."

Understanding the gravity of the situation, I mirrored his actions, closely watching for any signs of bears. I had gotten lucky on my first and only encounter with a bear, and I didn't want to chance that again.

Despite my expectation for small talk, Yu-jun seemed content with the peacefulness of the forest. I was unsure if that was because of a possible chance encounter with a four-legged creature or if he was just biding his time.

Upon returning to the hut, Yu-jun handed Ji the can of delicacies, and she began preparing our meal. During the wait, I inquired, "When should we leave tonight?"

Yu-jun responded, "When sun go down."

Wanting to be prepared, I asked, "Do you know which direction we're heading?"

Pointing toward my survival bag next to the door, he said, "I point."

I carefully unfolded the map across the table, drawing a disapproving look from Ji. Without a word, Yu-jun took the map from the table and placed it on the floor. As he studied the map intently, I pointed confidently to what I believed to be our approximate location, about three and a half miles from the border. Yu-jun nodded in agreement. Placing his finger on the map, He traced along the hills to the south. Clearly, he wanted to remain out of the valley too. Tapping his finger on a structure on the map, he said, "We go here to eat."

I nodded silently, conveying my understanding. The thought of visiting a building gave me pause as I was unsure if we should stop for a meal. My mind was running through all the risks associated with structures, because structures contained people. I kept my concerns to myself. It was clear that he was at a great risk as well. If it were found out that he and his sister were helping me, the consequences would be severe. I was sure the Army would not hesitate to execute them as well.

Heading south of the building, he gestured toward a spot just north of the border and announced, "We stay here tonight. I know a place."

Giving him a thumbs up, it appeared we would travel nearly two miles tonight and then attempt to cross the border the following night. I was uncertain of the time remaining before the Korean Army closed in on my location. With each passing day, the risk of being captured grew. We stepped outside and found Ji skillfully cooking over the fire pit. The aroma of her cooking was tantalizing, and I was eager to taste whatever she set before me.

Yu-jun expressed a keen interest in my family. I shared with him that my parents were hardworking farmers still living. We had a small farm with cows and a cornfield. I recounted my experiences of traveling across different states in my truck to visit parks and relatives. I could see the excitement in his eyes as he listened intently to every word I spoke.

Suddenly, he exclaimed, "I to be farmer and get a truck. Yes, I will do that in America."

His passion and determination were truly inspiring. His words spurred me on to do everything I could to ensure our safe passage across the border.

Ji signaled that it was time to eat, and we men sat down on the same two 5-gallon buckets. Ji placed two plates in front of us, and I couldn't help but feel that their cultural norms might not allow Ji to join us at the table. Nevertheless, I was committed to including her, so I gestured for Ji to grab another bucket and join us. She agreed, picked up a bucket from the corner of the hut, and sat beside her brother.

With our meal in front of us, I was taken aback by seeing both Yu-jun and Ji bowing their heads and uttering prayers in Korean. It dawned on me that I had previously observed them making the Catholic sign of the cross. Following their lead respectfully, I joined in the prayer, adding a few personal words before concluding with an

"Amen." As we raised our heads, our faces were adorned with radiant smiles. I felt an instant connection with these kindred spirits.

Ji's culinary skills surpassed all expectations as she worked her magic with the limited ingredients at her disposal. She transformed the boiled roots into delectable, medium-sized pancakes crowned with syrup from boiled raspberries. The resulting dish was divine, bursting with flavors, a pleasant surprise in the middle of nowhere. With the final bite, my shrunken stomach was thoroughly content, and the lingering sweet taste left a blissful sensation in my mouth.

With dinner finished, I toyed with the idea of taking a nap in the hammock, but my companions were busy gathering their things for our upcoming trip. I opted not to doze off under the trees, knowing I would have plenty of opportunities to rest soon. Instead, I observed them packing various items into a bag while discussing any last-minute necessities.

Venturing outside, I grabbed a cup and quenched my thirst with warm water until I couldn't drink anymore. Settling down next to the fire pit, my thoughts turned to my wife back in the States. I was certain that she had been informed of my aircraft accident, but she must have been feeling overwhelmed by the limited information. At least I had a sense of my surroundings and purpose. For her, the uncertainty must be unbearable. It seemed like a common experience for military spouses as their service members embarked on journeys to distant, foreign lands.

As they finished packing, Yu-jun emerged and sat down beside me on the ground. We sat silently, gazing at the dwindling sunlight peeking through the thick trees.

It was evident that something was troubling him; he couldn't find peace. Glancing at him, I saw him brush away a tear. He had always displayed bravery, but now the enormity of our undertaking seemed to hit him. I offered a smile and a reassuring thumbs-up. Whatever lay ahead, we were all in this together until the end.

After the sun disappeared, I carried the remaining water in the bucket to a patch of loose dirt. Mixing water with soil, I smeared the cool mud over my neck and face. Most of my golden attire now sported a dingy brown hue, with very few golden threads still visible.

I pulled up each sock, using tape from the first aid kit to secure them to my feet. Delighted that my socks had withstood my journey so far, I slathered on more mud until no white was visible.

After completing my task, I glanced up to find Yu-jun and Ji staring at me in astonishment at the transformation of my face. Yu-jun crouched down, smearing mud on his face and neck with evident enthusiasm. Ji, however, seemed resolute in her refusal to join us in applying dirt to her face. Chuckling to myself, I knew it had to be a boy thing.

We all rose to our feet and took a final look at the hut. Without ceremony, Yu-jun turned and started walking. I gestured for Ji to go next, and I followed closely behind.

As the darkness enveloped us, the only illumination was the faint light of the half-moon above. I was fortunate to have a little light from the moon every night. Yu-jun seemed unfazed by the darkness, appearing at ease as he moved beneath the leafy canopy. It dawned on me that his upbringing in the region had endowed him with an intimate knowledge of every path etched into the hillsides. We ascended one hill, descended into a valley with a meandering stream, and then ascended another. It was exhausting, but I had faith in their endurance and silently hoped that I could keep pace with my younger newfound friends.

We had been traveling for a while, and it became difficult to gauge the distance we had covered. I signaled to Yu-jun that we should take a break. There was no point in pushing ourselves too hard and risking injury. Yu-jun agreed, and we took a ten-minute break, during which I drank some water from my container. I noticed they didn't have any water and offered mine. They accepted, and drank sparingly. I sensed water was not a big concern for them since we had already crossed two streams. I was sure Yu-jun knew how to procure water across these hills any time he needed.

After our break, we continued to move forward in single file for about an hour before taking another rest. I checked my watch and saw that it was 12:45 at night. The lack of sufficient rest during the day was beginning to take its toll on me. I could feel my energy levels dropping even with my extra nutrition. My breathing was also becoming more labored. I was not used to this fast pace.

Yu-jun noticed me slowing down. Looking at me, he said, "Almost there."

I was unsure of where "there" was, but I assumed it was the building he had pointed out on the map. Despite my uncertainty about our destination, I had to trust Yu-jun; he had brought me this far.

After a brief rest, I signaled to Yu-jun that I was ready to continue. He took the lead, with Ji close behind. Despite being half my age, the two showed marvelous, focused determination, with no complaints. They trekked through the terrain with a resolve that I found admirable.

As we veered off the trail, we descended into the denser woods. Our pace slowed considerably as prickly bushes and thorns hindered our progress. While the siblings seemed to navigate the obstacles effortlessly, I found myself continually grappling with the treacherous thorns that latched onto my hands and clothes.

As we ventured farther down the hill, we stumbled upon a seemingly out-of-place light blue building. Upon spotting it, Yu-jun motioned for me to crouch and remain still. I followed his lead and watched as they both proceeded toward the building.

Sitting myself next to a large rock, I saw the two of them disappear around the front of the structure. Some inscriptions adorned the side of the building, but they were illegible from my vantage point.

There was nothing for me to do but wait for their return. I wasn't particularly thirsty, and there was no need to consult the map. As seconds stretched into minutes and then further into more minutes, impatience got the better of me. I rose to my feet, inching closer to the building. I attempted to locate a window but to no avail. Retrieving my penlight, I tried to decipher the inscriptions on the side of the building. The symbols were in Korean, with a cross featured below, indicating that it was a church. Perhaps a Catholic Church I thought, given Yu-jun and Ji's past actions.

As I cautiously peeked around the front corner, a gentle

solar ground light cast a soft glow on a three-foot wooden statue of Mary, confirming my suspicions. I carefully retreated to my hiding spot, determined to remain unseen as I waited.

Half an hour later, they both returned, carrying food. Yu-jun kindly offered me some bread and rice, as we sat quietly under the twinkling stars.

After eating, I tended to my socks, re-taping them. I could feel the holes forming at the bottom, exposing the leather to the ground. Despite their rank odor, the inside pair of socks were holding up surprisingly well.

After eating, we set off on our journey again. As Yu-jun walked past me, I noticed an old western-style six-shooter attached to his belt. The black gun sported a beautiful ivory handle. Having a weapon gave me a slight sense of relief, knowing that we had some form of protection, but with only six shots, it was evident we would be outgunned. I also wondered about Yu-jun's experience with firearms and if he had ever shot a gun before. For that matter, I wasn't even sure if the gun was loaded.

As we traveled, the trees started to thin out, and I felt a keen sense of unease seeing how close we were to the valley floor. Despite my concerns, I remained silent and let Yu-jun continue leading us. We took two more breaks before reaching a section of the forest dotted with large round boulders.

Climbing upon the highest boulder, Yu-jun pointed off in the distance. "The border is two hills over. Tomorrow, we cross," he stated.

Wow! I couldn't believe how far we had come. The line

between freedom and captivity was considerably closer now. The urge to run and cross the border tonight was almost overwhelming, but I knew it would be reckless. I prayed that Yu-jun had a solid plan for the most challenging part of our –journey—the last mile.

At Yu-jun's direction, we backtracked to the center of the boulders, carefully snaking our way through a narrow entrance into a sheltered area nestled within the rock formation. The time was 3:45 in the morning.

I was overwhelmed with exhaustion, craving some much-needed rest. Tomorrow promised to be physically demanding, and I was determined to conserve every last bit of energy. Meanwhile, Yu-jun and Ji retrieved a small blanket from their bag and spread it on the ground. I chose to lean against a small tree that had taken root beside one of the boulders. Placing my survival kit at the base of the tree, I used it as a pillow as I lay on the barren ground. Looking to the stars in heaven, I took a moment to contemplate the day I'd just had. It started off in a blueberry patch and ended surrounded by boulders with two new companions. Who would have guessed?

CHAPTER 6

The Rescue

I sensed a gentle nudge against the sole of my foot. Gradually opening my eyes, I gazed up at the brilliant sky. However, the nudging persisted, becoming more insistent. As I focused, I was startled to come face to face with two men kneeling beside me, their faces concealed by carefully blended camouflage bandanas. I tried to move, but my body felt unresponsive. Meeting the gaze of the closest man, I noticed that he was not Korean but American.

Realizing that I was awake, he gestured for me to remain silent with a finger to his lips. Then, using the same hand, he pointed toward Yu-jun and Ji, still deep in sleep. The man subsequently made a thumbs-up and then a thumbs-down sign with his hand, silently asking whether they were friend or foe. I considered his unspoken question odd, considering we were all in the same resting spot. I raised my hand and returned the thumbs-up gesture. The man acknowledged my gesture.

I slowly sat up, taking in a few deep breaths. Gently, I

reached out and shook Yu-jun's leg, hoping he wouldn't startle and reach for the gun lying nearby, leading to a disastrous outcome. When his eyes opened, I pressed my finger to my lips, silently urging him to remain quiet.

Carefully shifting my position so that Yu-jun could see, I gestured toward the two military men and whispered, "They're Americans. They're here to help us."

A bright smile spread across Yu-jun's face as he gently shook his sister to wake her. As she stirred, he murmured to her in Korean, and she turned to see the newcomers. Ji waved to the strangers, one of the few signs of emotion I had seen out of her.

Turning my attention to our new friends, I inquired, "Are you guys Navy Seals?"

The man shook his head and replied, "No. We're Air Force pararescue. I'm Sergeant Kurt Rodriguez," gesturing behind him, he said, "This is Sergeant Jack Maze."

With a grin, I exclaimed, "I can't believe the military sent you across the border to get me!"

Sergeant Rodriguez approached me quietly, trying to keep our conversation hushed. He was short and stocky, with arms as big as my legs. He was built like a brick wall. In contrast, Sergeant Maze appeared to be a lot taller with a more slender build.

Since Rodriguez took the lead in the conversation, I speculated he was the higher-ranking of the two. Both men were heavily camouflaged, making it challenging to make out their facial features, except for the whites of their eyes.

With a subtle smile, Rodriguez responded, "They didn't

force us to come; we volunteered." Upon hearing this, Maze let out a chuckle. Rodriguez then turned his attention to Yu-jun and Ji and remarked, "Our protocol dictates bringing only you back. We can't bring those two along."

Initially uncertain how to react, I quickly realized that it was essential to convey that Yu-jun understood most of what was being said. I informed them, "He speaks English."

Rodriguez shrugged and stated, "We still can't take them with us."

Taking a deep breath, I knew I had to keep my promise. Meeting Rodriguez's gaze, I firmly asserted, "They're coming with me. I wouldn't be here without their assistance. I pledged to get them to America if they helped me cross the border, and I will not go back on my word."

Considering the unexpected turn of events, Rodriguez exchanged glances with Maze. With a look of indifference, Maze shrugged, "Do we have a choice?"

"No," I replied firmly before Rodriguez could say anything. I wanted to end any thought of leaving the Koreans behind.

Rodriguez appeared somewhat dejected as he weighed my new demand, "Okay. I'll notify rescue that five of us will be coming across tonight."

Observing the two men and their gear, I noticed both were equipped with earpieces connected to concealed transmitters. They were armed with the latest military Sig Sauer XM7 assault rifles, mounted scopes and extra magazines protruding from their belts. They were heavily armed and ready for a firefight if needed.

Rodriguez ordered Maze to take up a lookout position at the top of the boulders.

The arrival of our guests filled me with hope, knowing that our odds of survival had significantly improved. Glancing at Yu-jun and Ji, I saw that they closely observed my reaction. I responded with another thumbs-up and a wide smile. Yu-jun smiled back, and they both settled back down.

"Sergeant Rodriguez, what time can we expect our extraction?" I inquired.

Rodriguez paused for a moment before responding. It was clear that he was cautiously considering how much information he should reveal in the presence of the nearby Koreans. "They're okay," I assured him.

Finally relenting, he disclosed, "0200 hours."

"Copy," I acknowledged. Trying to lighten the mood, I inquired, "Where are you guys from?"

"I'm from Lawton, Utah, and Jack is from Elk Creek, Kentucky," answered Rodriguez. Despite his lack of interest in casual conversation, I persisted, asking, "How did you both manage to cross the border?"

With a smirk, he replied, "Last night, we had a 2 a.m. go time. We parachuted out of the back of a C-130 with winged parachutes two miles south of the DMZ at 10,000 feet. Our landing zone was half a mile behind your last reported position, so we had to fly over three miles in the chutes to get to you."

Astonished, I responded, "You were able to track me?"

"Yes," he continued, "We've been monitoring your movements with three infrared satellites since your ejection. We first detected your landing by the lake. After a day of losing sight of you, we spotted you swimming across the lake. We suspected it was you using the signaling mirror on the South Korean fighters. Intel confirmed your location, and the Air Force asked for volunteers to parachute in and assist with your extraction. Jack and I stepped up. We've maintained constant communication with Intel, who provided real-time updates on your movements throughout the night, guiding us to your present location. Two extraction teams are poised to meet at our crossing point tonight."

I marveled at their impressive tracking capability and found solace in the fact that the enemy didn't possess such advanced means. Despite my exhaustion, sleep beckoned. Observing my weariness, Rodriguez offered, "Get some rest. We'll depart at midnight for a 2 a.m. extraction. We'll be keeping watch over everyone."

Agreeing with his suggestion, I rested my head on my survival kit again and closed my eyes. A whirlwind of emotion raced through my mind, and it took some time for my excitement to subside. Eventually, I drifted to sleep.

Stirring once from the oppressive stillness with the cluster of boulders blocking any breeze, I spotted Rodriguez perched atop the rocks. At the same time, Maze was reclined against the same boulder near me. I made a concerted effort to force myself to continue sleeping, trying to preserve my energy if possible.

Approaching 6 p.m., I could not sleep anymore. I awoke to find several protein bars and three small Mylar bags of water by my side. Yu-jun and Ji also had a half-dozen bars and some water beside them. After consuming all the bars, I drank two waters.

Time seemed to stop. We lay there in silence as daylight waned into darkness. Suddenly, the screeching of brakes reverberated off the surrounding rocks, making it difficult to discern the location of the noise.

Observing Rodriguez, I noticed that he was lying flat against the rocks and using hand signals to communicate with Maze. I couldn't comprehend their signs; all I could do was wait for an explanation.

Maze kept his gaze fixed on his partner perched above. When Maze shifted his focus to me, I inquired, "What's happening?"

He explained that two North Korean jeeps and a troop personnel carrier were stopped on the road just thirty yards below us.

Not knowing what would come next, Yu-jun approached me, seeking any information. I explained to him everything I knew. Meanwhile, Ji sat crouched in a ball, visibly distressed as she rocked back and forth, her arms clinging to her legs.

In a surprising move, Yu-jun pointed to his chest and uttered, "I will fix," before swiftly exiting the entrance.

Despite Maze's attempt to intervene, Yu-jun managed to slip past him and proceeded into the woods on a mission. Puzzled by his actions, I had no idea what Yu-jun was up to. I wished he would have consulted us first.

Maze was visibly disturbed and said, "You sure you trust this kid?"

As tension mounted, the question of trust hung heavy in the air. I responded unequivocally, "Yes, I do. Why would he leave his sister if he was going to give our position up?"

Grinding his teeth, Maze was upset that Yu-jun had got past him. He responded, "I hope you're right; otherwise, we're going to have a nasty fight on our hands."

I noticed Rodriguez positioned on the rock, communicating with Maze. His expression seemed extremely troubled. Maze, in response, made several reassuring hand gestures, which appeared to alleviate Rodriguez's concerns.

We all stood silently, straining our ears for any noises that might provide clues. No one dared to speak for what felt like an eternity. Finally, we discerned a man shouting orders from the nearby road, followed by trucks setting into motion. That had to be a promising sign, I told myself.

We endured ten long minutes before Yu-jun returned to our hiding place. I warmly greeted him with a broad smile and asked, "What did you do?"

"I told them someone sleeping in woods back by the blue building. Maybe be person they look for," Yu-jun said, smiling.

Maze acknowledged I was correct and expressed his gratitude, saying, "Good call. Get some rest. We leave in two hours."

The wait felt like an eternity as we sat in the darkness, bracing ourselves for our impending departure. My mind drifted back to thoughts of my wife. I pondered whether she had been informed about the rescue operation tonight. It seemed unlikely, as the military only disclosed information to those deemed with "the need to know." I figured my squadron mates probably knew. They would have demanded to be kept up to date on everything.

At midnight, Rodriguez descended from the boulder and inquired if we were ready to go. Yu-jun and I confirmed our readiness, and Ji nodded. "Okay, follow closely behind me and maintain absolute silence," Rodriguez ordered.

I murmured to myself, "It's showtime, Dan. You can do this."

Rodriguez led the way, trailed closely by Yu-jun and Ji. I found myself in the middle, with Maze bringing up the rear. We navigated the forest for about 150 yards before Rodriguez signaled us to halt by raising his hand. Even Yu-jun and Ji understood the significance of the hand gesture.

As the sounds of the forest filled the air, Rodriguez focused intently on the front of the group while Maze kept a vigilant watch behind us. Witnessing the skills of these professionals firsthand was something I had previously seen only in movies. Watching them in action was even more impressive. Rodriguez then gave the "all clear" and we proceeded again.

After a while, we came across a small stream intersecting our path. Rodriguez stopped us and advised, "This may be our last chance for water. Drink up as much as you can. I don't want anyone getting dehydrated." The two Koreans and I eagerly drank from the semi-cool water, which helped to calm our frayed nerves.

Meanwhile, Rodriguez and Maze examined their map, exchanging in a quiet conversation. I took comfort in their confidence, reassured that we were in capable hands. Our break concluded, and we embarked on another uphill climb, hoping it would be the final ascent. However, as we reached the peak, another hill loomed ahead, testing the limits of our eagerness to get to the border.

On the next hill, Rodriguez raised his hand for us to freeze. We immediately obeyed. As we reached the crest of the hill, he gestured for us to remain quiet and signaled us to move in slow motion. We sensed that we were getting close to the border. The silence was so profound that I couldn't tell if Maze was still trailing behind me.

We proceeded cautiously, taking a few steps, halting, and then a few more steps. This careful progression was repeated a dozen times until Rodriguez directed us to hold our position. After scanning the area below him, he motioned for us to come closer to his position. When we gathered around him, he whispered, "From here on out, no talking. Watch my hand signals and follow my lead. Lt. Colonel Preston, you follow behind me; the two Koreans will follow you, and Maze will bring up the rear. Any questions?"

I disagreed with the proposed order. I worried that Yujun and Ji might be vulnerable if hostilities erupted. This was unacceptable to me, and I was determined to convey this to Rodriguez. "No, Ji should follow you and then her brother. I will follow as number four with Maze behind me." Pointing to the two Koreans, I stated, "I want them in front of me, not behind me."

I found myself in another tense situation with Rodriguez, expecting an argument. Much surprised, he replied, "Have it your way."

I felt a rush of gratitude while getting Ji and Yu-jun's attention. I pointed to Rodriguez and raised one finger. I then pointed to Ji with two fingers and Yu-jun with three. I used four fingers to represent myself and five for Maze. Confirming their comprehension, I gave them a thumbs-up, and they reciprocated, acknowledging that they had understood who to follow.

As we prepared to move, Maze approached me and directed, "You need to get rid of the survival kit. We have to go under the wire."

Taking Maze's suggestion to heart, I unstrapped the kit from my back. I pondered whether there was anything I should keep in my pockets for later use. After mentally recalling each item in the kit, I couldn't find a compelling reason to hold onto anything, so I discreetly stashed the kit in some underbrush. Those contents were my sole possessions for the past few days, representing the only items I had for my survival.

I gripped my penlight tightly and checked my watch. Suddenly, Maze tapped me on the shoulder and shook his head, indicating I had made a mistake. I felt frustrated with myself for such a foolish error. At that moment, I realized that the time was their concern, not mine.

We proceeded carefully, stepping into each other's footprints as we descended. The low hum of a distant generator helped drown any noises we might have made. My nerves were on edge with each step, but I reassured myself that each one brought us closer to freedom.

As we drew nearer, the terrain became less rugged. Rodriguez used a GPS monitor to guide us to the exact location where we needed to be. He adjusted our course to the left for the final 100 yards. Now, we were just a few feet from the clearing.

I could sense an open space beyond the few trees before us, but I couldn't see the wire fence yet. Rodriguez gestured for us to stay put as he moved forward cautiously. Meanwhile, Maze kept a watchful eye on Rodriguez from our position while swiveling his head backward to monitor our rear.

We remained crouched in our hidden position, straining to see any signs from Rodriguez. I could have cut the tension with a knife as my knees began to protest the uncomfortable position. I shifted my weight subtly to alleviate the discomfort, all the while acutely aware of my thundering heartbeat, fearing that it would betray our presence to the North Koreans.

Maze and Rodriguez were busy exchanging cryptic hand signals as the Koreans and I waited for the translations. Then, another round of gestures ensued, culminating in Maze raising two fingers to alert us. Two minutes to showtime. I observed Maze produce wire cutters from a concealed pocket in his pants.

Time stretched on. I strained to peer ahead, witnessing Rodriguez pressing his hand to his earpiece and whispering into the microphone. Suddenly, two muted pops interrupted the ambient hum of the generator, so subtle that only those anticipating the sounds would have detected them.

Rodriguez gestured swiftly for us to follow, and Maze repeated the signal to ensure we understood. With each deliberate step, I trailed behind Yu-jun as we entered the clearing. Suddenly, the intimidating sight of galvanized razor wire appeared twenty yards before us. The rolls of wire, stacked up to 15 feet high, loomed over us, clearly designed to deter anyone or anything from attempting to navigate through it. The sharp, pointed edges of the wire glistened in the moonlight, ready to ensnare and tear apart any clothing or flesh that dared to come into contact with it.

As I glanced to my left, the moonlight revealed two motionless bodies, the unfortunate victims of the sniper shots. I wondered how many snipers were positioned on the other side of the fence. Despite the unease, I found comfort in the thought that they were vigilantly watching over us, ready to neutralize any potential threats without hesitation.

Rodriguez crouched down as he carefully reached the razor wire, steadily beginning to cut through it. The rest of us dropped to our knees in the exposed area, ready to follow Rodriguez. The tension in the wire would release with each wire snipped, creating a sharp "twang" that echoed through the air. Rodriguez worked as quickly as he could, but it was clear that it would take some time to get through all the wire. At least 20 feet of wire lay along the ground, creating a formidable barrier we had to navigate carefully.

As the process dragged on longer than I had anticipated, we found ourselves exposed and vulnerable in the open. Then, out of the corner of my eye, I noticed the outline of a person on the South Korean side of the wire. To my surprise, he began cutting through the wire on that side, intending to meet us in the middle.

Rodriguez carefully cut through the first few feet of wire, then shifted his position to lie on his back. He meticulously kept cutting the wires above his head. After each cut, he would maneuver his body a few more inches through the tangled mesh of wires. Each cut was one step closer to South Korea.

Ji carefully rolled onto her back, keeping close to Rodriguez's heels. The silent night was punctuated only by the rhythmic sounds of the cutters working away, followed by the unmistakable twang each wire made. I could only guess that there had to be a hundred wires that needed to be cut, and some even twice, as they shifted.

Two minutes later, Yu-jun turned onto his back and followed behind his sister. I was next in line. I quickly glanced to my right and left, hoping to catch any movement, but the surroundings remained quiet. My chest ached with pulsating pain, and it felt as though my heart were on the verge of bursting. For a split second, the terrifying thought of experiencing a heart attack flashed through my mind.

Finally, it was my turn. I rolled onto my back and started to scoot back and forth in the sandy bottom, trying to stay close to Yu-jun. The razor wire swayed above our heads as one piece nailed my left hand. The pain was not immediate, but seconds later, I felt it. The nasty wire was deadly.

The slow pace made it clear that we were all struggling with the razor wire snapping back at us whenever we made another cut. Then, a strand of wire grabbed my arm like an octopus tentacle. I lifted the taut wire a couple of inches to clear my arm of the deadly metal. With that wire out of the way, I could move a few more inches toward freedom. Our movement now was defined by inches.

As I twisted my neck to look in front of me, I saw Yu-jun struggling with a smaller, round, delicate wire. This wire was different from the razor wire above us. This wire seemed hidden in the sand for some reason and had become entangled with his belt and pistol grip. As Yu-jun tugged at the wire to free himself, a deafening explosion echoed through the air.

Immediately, shrapnel from the claymore mine 15 feet to my right pelted my entire chest and right arm. The explosion left us all in a daze. I knew I was alive because of the pain, but I was unsure if I had all of my body parts. There were no sounds from the others. Dust and smoke filled the air, making it hard to breathe and see.

A bright spotlight appeared to my left on the North Korean side of the border, trying to cut through the haze. Then I heard Rodriguez shout, "Target left."

Then, a single muffled pop rang out, and the light disappeared. Loud, repeating "rat-a-tat-tat-tat-tat," machine gun fire began to my right. A 50-caliber was taking aim at us as the haze began to dissipate. I could see tracers methodically walking to our position, just above our heads.

"Machine gun, east," Rodriguez screamed, followed by another single muffled pop, and the 50-caliber went silent. Continuing to give orders, Rodriguez yelled at us, "We need to move now."

We hurried as swiftly as possible, skillfully moving through the dense web of deadly wire. The explosion from the Claymore had repositioned some wires, creating a small gap for us to maneuver. I could see Rodriguez, Ji, and Yu-jun breaking free from the entanglement. As I neared the last stretch of wire, a sudden "twang" echoed through the air, and a lengthy strand of razor wire hooked onto my left upper thigh.

The wire was so taut I could not slide my leg under it. As I grabbed the wire with both hands, I could feel blood oozing, making my grip slippery. The wire was just too tight. As I glanced upward, I noticed Rodriguez and Yu-jun grabbing a hold of my outer garment to pull me out when a deafening blast from another 50-caliber machine gun erupted nearby.

"Get down," Rodriguez cried as he flattened himself on the ground.

Yu-jun kept pulling on my garment when I screamed, "Get down, Yu-jun! Get down!"

The tracers flew inches above my head when Yu-jun jolted backward, letting go of my garment. Sitting on the ground stunned, he had taken a bullet through the right side of his chest.

Rodriguez screamed again in the microphone, and the machine gun went silent.

"No. No. No," I screamed at the top of my lungs. I could see Yu-jun's wide, glossy eyes with his mouth open. In shock, he just stared straight ahead. His breathing was raspy as he spit up a small amount of blood.

Then I felt Rodriguez grab both my arms and yell, "I'm going to pull you out."

I could feel the full power of those gigantic arms, and he pulled my body toward him. I felt the razor wire cutting through my clothing and skin, as Rodriguez pulled with all his might. The moment I was free, the pain of the razor wire hit with full force. I gritted my teeth and tightened all my stomach muscles as I thought I was going to pass out. I had never felt such pain in my life before. Previous broken bones were no comparison.

I could hear Ji screaming in the distance, as Yu-jun was still sitting in the same position, trying to breathe. Rodriguez hoisted me over his shoulder and began moving into the woods while screaming orders into the microphone. He yelled for Maze to grab the Korean boy. I could hear more machine gun fire in the distance as illumination flares crisscrossed the sky. The night became day within seconds.

Straddling Rodriguez's sturdy shoulders, I felt him navigate our way into a secluded, sheltered valley 50 yards away from the wire. Suddenly, I found myself being hoisted onto a flatbed truck. Two unfamiliar faces carefully laid me down and immediately started tending to my injuries.

A female medic, devoid of camouflage, swiftly began cutting away my clothing to access the wound on my left leg. Another figure, a Korean Army medic, administered a needle in my right thigh, remarking, "Welcome to Heartbreak Ridge, South Korea."

Just then, Maze hoisted up Yu-jun on the flatbed on my left. I rolled my head to see Yu-jun. He was looking directly at me. His eyes were still wide open, but with a blank stare.

The Korean medic moved over to straddle Yu-jun's chest. Intertwining his fingers, he gave a single chest compression to Yu-jun. Blood spurted out of the hole in his chest onto my body. I knew that was a bad sign.

Straight away, the Korean medic knew it was hopeless and ceased compressions.

In a weak voice, I said, "Don't stop. Keep trying." I started feeling the effects of pain medicine from the shot.

The medic glanced at me, shook his head, and said, "I'm sorry, he's gone. His lungs have been punctured. I wish there was something I could do, but it's too late." The devastating news broke my heart, along with my promise.

The truck slowly began to move along the road, but my gaze was fixed on Yu-jun. His expression remained frozen, his eyes wide open, as if he were trying to say something to me. He gave his life trying to help me. Tears filled my eyes as I whispered, "I'm sorry, Yu-jun. I'm so sorry I couldn't keep my promise."

As we jostled along for another minute, drowsiness slowly crept over me. Illumination from the flares continued, reminiscent of a Fourth of July celebration in America. I could hear the whooshing sound of helicopter blades as the truck came to a stop. Try as I might, I couldn't keep my eyes open any longer.

CHAPTER 7

Going Home

I could hear faint voices in the background but could not muster up the effort to open my eyes. I felt a comforting hand covering the top of mine. My brain was registering a throbbing sensation erupting from all parts of my body. It felt like someone had hit me repeatedly with a baseball bat. Pain sensors in my brain were overloaded.

"Honey, can you hear me?" a voice I instantly recognized.

"I can hear you," I said, but no sound came from my mouth. My lips seemed paralyzed as I tried to speak. Trying with all my might, I could not make any sound. My eyes would not open, seemingly glued shut. Struggling, I blinked as hard as I could. Finally, one eyelid relinquished. Blinking several more times, the other one followed. The images before me were blurry. The more I blinked, the more focused the images became. I saw a woman with reddish-blond hair wearing glasses.

It was my precious wife, Jewel. My eyes continued to clear.

I could see her wiping away the tears. Streaks of makeup left lines on her face. A nurse in the background raised her hand to her mouth and, without a sound, left the room. I saw clear plastic tubes above my head, twisting down onto my right arm, feeding me fluids of some kind.

"Dan, can you hear?" Jewel asked again, this time louder.

Gently nodding, I mustered up a weak voice, and replied, "Yeah."

An overjoyed smile lit up her face as she said, "Everything will be alright. You are in the hospital. The doctors and nurses have taken good care of you. We're just so thankful you're alive!"

Visions of the last week raced through my mind as I tried to piece together the events. I remembered having to eject out of the airplane, but I couldn't recall why. I also remembered running through the woods, desperately trying to get somewhere. Some of my memories were returning, while other parts were still fuzzy.

My thoughts were interrupted as my discomfort returned. The sharp sting in my left leg felt like a hot poker pressing into my skin. More pain came from my right arm, but not as severe as my leg. Everything was throbbing. Did I get shot? I couldn't recall, and the pieces were not falling into place quickly enough.

"What happened?" I muttered softly.

My wife closed both eyes as tears continued streaming down her cheeks. Squeezing my hand tighter, she said, "I am not exactly sure, but they told me there was a land mine that exploded when you were trying to get across the border. They've pulled a lot of shrapnel out of you. It will take some time for you to heal, but the doctors expect a full recovery."

Her words stirred my recollection. Pictures of the two Korean teenagers and the pararescue men flashed by. I remembered we were all crawling under the barbed wire when I blurted out, "Did the Korean boy make it?"

Squeezing her lips together, she shook her head and said, "No, they couldn't save him, but the young girl is okay."

My heart sank as I remembered seeing Yu-jun's blank stare at me. He had made the ultimate sacrifice to get across the border. The dream of escaping the oppression of North Korea and living a better life was all he wanted. My heart sank as he would not see that dream come true.

Gazing at my beautiful wife, I asked, "How did you get here so fast?"

She smiled and replied, "Dan, you've been sleeping for four days. I've been here in Korea for the last two days. I haven't left your side since arriving."

I was stunned by the realization of my prolonged slumber; a void opened within me. It felt as if I had missed out on so much. Never before had I slept for such an extended period. Yet, I was alive, and that was a comforting thought. As vitality returned through my veins, I cautiously flexed my toes and fingers, ensuring their functionality. They responded, but every bone in my body throbbed with agony.

The door to my room opened. A distinguished older gentleman in a white uniform with matching hair appeared with a stethoscope around his neck. "Hi, I'm Doctor Bishop. How are you feeling today?" he asked while using one hand to pull his glasses from the top of his head onto his face.

"Everything hurts like hell, doc," I responded.

Raising the collar of my gown so I could see my chest, he said, "Understandable. As you can see, we pulled two dozen pieces of shrapnel out of your body."

As I looked down at my torso, I noticed numerous white gauze pads, each fastened to my body with tape.

"The largest piece of shrapnel hit your right arm, but it will heal with time. You also had a deep cut from your left knee down to your ankle," the doctor explained. "We stitched that up and covered it with some clear new skin. Take it easy on that cut; it was deep, and we had to use a lot of stitches."

I could see through the transparent glue applied over the two-foot cut. The black stitches formed a crisscross pattern along the entire length of the gash. Looking at my injury, flashbacks of Rodriguez and Yu-jun pulling on my garment resurfaced.

Holding his stethoscope, the doctor listened to my heart while glancing at a machine displaying my vitals. "You lost a lot of blood and probably some weight. Take it easy and give yourself a chance to heal. We should have you out of here in a few days. I'll be back to check on you. Do you have any questions?" he asked.

I shook my head and gave him a thumbs-up, indicating no questions. "Thanks, doc," I said as he turned and left the room.

As the doctor exited, Jewel poked her head out the door and was conversing with someone on the other side. Just then, the trio of Brady, Terry, and Grover strolled through the door.

With a warm smile, Grover extended his hand and asked, 'Hey buddy, how are you holding up?'

I pressed the up button on my hospital bed and replied, "I think I'll live. Not sure I want to come back to work anytime soon."

All three men laughed together. "Well, it's good to see you. We missed you, and I can't imagine what you went through," Grover said.

"Yeah, I don't want to do that again," I said with a smile. "I have no idea what went wrong with the plane. All of a sudden, everything just went haywire."

"We figured it out while you were gallivanting around North Korea," Grover responded cheerfully while gesturing toward Brady.

Brady then placed a black, boomerang looking metal piece on my lap. I picked it up and examined it before saying, "This looks like an antenna off of the airplane."

"It is," Brady replied. "That's why your screens went blank, and the autopilot followed a new navigation point sent to your aircraft. That's how your plane ended up crossing the border."

Still not fully comprehending, I asked, "How did you get this off my plane?"

"We didn't," Brady retorted. "We got it off the other U-2. We've been busy day and night since your ejection. First, we meticulously dissected your conversation with the Link personnel before you ejected. We found it peculiar that you noticed a DownLink Control light on the aircraft just before your screens went blank. Second, we all remembered that you had spotted the same DownLink Control light during the preflight of my flight a few days earlier. This was too much of a coincidence, so we figured something was amiss."

Brady pressed on, his finger pointing at Terry. "Terry decided to investigate if our secure link had been hacked and if someone was manipulating the plane using our frequencies."

Terry smiled from ear to ear, proud of his investigating prowess. I struggled to process the whirlwind of new information. They had been tirelessly working while I was absent, and the implications of their discoveries were staggering.

Terry took over the story and explained, "I collaborated with the head Lockheed representative, Tom Romero, to thoroughly inspect the other aircraft to see if that aircraft could provide any insights or failures of our systems. That's when we discovered someone had installed a fake antenna on that plane too. This fake antenna," Terry said, pointing to the antenna in my hand. "Was directly connected to the DownLink Control system. It could take control of certain systems in the aircraft when triggered by a rogue ground signal."

I was slow to process everything, and Terry paused for a second to let everything he said sink in.

"After obtaining this information," Terry continued, "we had our intelligence team scan the entire peninsula for any unauthorized signals that could reach the aircraft. A day later, our Intel informed us that a Rivet Joint KC-135 aircraft had detected a transmission coming from a location near our base."

I found their discoveries very intriguing, and I felt relieved that I had not made any mistakes that resulted in the loss of an aircraft in North Korea.

Brady took over the story and said, "Once we located the transmission, we informed the Office of Special Investigations from the base. The OSI raided the house but the occupant had already left. During the raid, they discovered that one of our Lockheed representatives, Ted Ross, was renting the house."

Brady reached behind him, pulled out a silver metal box, and said, "This is what the OSI found buried in the backyard. It's a homemade transmitter, powerful enough to send signals to the plane even at altitude."

"I recognize that box," I exclaimed, my voice filled with shock.

"What!" Brady yelled, his surprise written over his face.

"Yes, I saw a technician with that box the morning I was conducting the preflight check on your aircraft when I encountered all the problems with the DownLink Control light."

I could tell this was a piece of the puzzle the boys did not have. Nodding with a smirk, Brady responded, "He must have been testing it out when you were doing the preflight on my plane."

"So, let me get this straight. This Lockheed technician was transmitting signals to my aircraft, causing my systems to go haywire?" I asked, trying to wrap my head around the situation. "Why?"

Grover stepped closer and replied, "I had just fired

him that morning before your flight for defrauding the government by submitting fake invoices. I had him escorted off the base, revoked his credentials, and informed Lockheed back in the States of our actions. We believe he knew he was going to get fired and wanted payback, so he likely activated his device while you were airborne. We're unsure if he intended to crash the plane, but that's irrelevant. OSI later discovered that he had purchased a plane ticket back to the States the day after your crash. We notified the State Department and the Defense Department of our suspicions, and they issued a warrant for his arrest. The FBI located him in Mexico yesterday, and they are in the process of bringing him back to the States now."

I was genuinely amazed at the talent of my squadron mates. "And you all figured this out on your own?" I asked.

The three men smiled from ear to ear simultaneously. Then, Grover nodded and replied, "It was a team effort. Each of us seemed to have a piece of the puzzle, and once we shared our pieces, the picture became a little clearer."

"Wow. I'm impressed. I thought I was going crazy when I first saw that DownLink Control light on during the preflight. I was even starting to question myself," I responded.

Grover patted me on the shoulder, saying, "Anyway, get some rest. We can talk later, but you need to spend some time with your wife. We have you both booked on a United flight back to the States in three days."

"Boss, I can't thank you enough for all you've done," I expressed with genuine gratitude.

Grover acknowledged my compliment and asked, "Do you need anything before we go?"

As the boys were about to part ways, my stomach let out a loud rumble, reminding me I had neglected it for too long. "If it's not too much trouble, I would really like some steak and eggs from the chow hall," I requested. Hunger was evident in my voice.

"You got it, buddy. How do you want the steak cooked?" Grover replied.

That brought a chuckle from Brady and me while Grover and Terry looked baffled. "I'll take the steak well done and the eggs scrambled if that is okay?" If you can't beat them, I thought you might as well join them.

Without knowing about the inside joke, Grover smiled and replied, "Be back in a bit." I felt grateful for Grover's willingness to secure me something other than hospital food.

After my buddies left, Jewel came back in, and we talked briefly before I succumbed to sleep again. I had never felt so tired in my life.

As the afternoon wore on, I was roused from my slumber by my wife's unexpected news that two men from the U.S. government were here to see me.

Two impeccably dressed men, with a striking resemblance that could have mistaken them for twins, entered my room. Their all-black jackets, ties, and pants stood in contrast to their white shirts, reminiscent of the iconic Men in Black movie, and immediately signaled their affiliation with a three-letter government agency. I tried with all my might not to laugh, as that would be ill-advised in my condition.

With a steady voice, the taller of the two men spoke first. "Lt. Colonel Preston, I'm Tim Bennett, and this is James Fredrick. We're from the Defense Intelligence Agency and are here to accompany your return to the States. We'll also conduct a debriefing once we get back regarding your mishap in North Korea."

Instantly, I had a bad feeling about these two men as my ears perked up. What did they mean by my mishap in North Korea? It sounded like they thought I had intentionally crossed some line in the dirt to create an international incident. I was in no mood to get a lecture from these two idiots.

I studied Mr. Bennett's face for a long five seconds before responding. Annoyed, I asked, "What about the girl? Has she made it to the States yet?"

Shaking his head, Bennett responded, "No, she will have to stay in South Korea since she illegally crossed their border. She's in their custody now."

I carefully considered his statement and calculated my options for my next move. Ji and her brother risked their lives to help me cross the DMZ, so I owed it to her to at least try to ensure that her dream would still come true.

"The girl needs to go back to the States with my wife and me, where she will be sworn in as a U.S. citizen when we arrive," I stated bluntly.

Raising his eyebrows, I saw my brazen request had taken Mr. Bennett aback. Bennett shook his head and responded, "Absolutely not. She is the responsibility of the South Koreans now."

I could feel my blood boiling and was sure my vital monitors above me reflected the same information. I had nothing to lose and all the cards to play.

"If that girl is not on the plane with my wife and me, then there will be no debriefing. Do you understand that? Second, if she is not granted American citizenship, I will be talking to the news organizations about your horrible treatment of me and the girl. Do I make myself clear?"

Bennett looked like he had seen a ghost. At this point, he also realized I held all the cards, and he was at my mercy. Partly relenting, he said, "I will make some calls and see what I can do. I can't guarantee anything."

With a confident smirk, I replied, "I'm sure you can make it happen." Maintaining my upper hand, I asked, "Where is the boy's body?"

"They buried him in a cemetery in Seoul yesterday," Bennett replied.

"I want to see his grave before our flight back to the States," I demanded.

Yielding to yet another of my demands, Bennett replied, "Alright, we can do that."

"I appreciate that," I responded, a hint of a smile playing on my lips as I motioned to the men that our conversation was over.

Once the two men left, I started taking deep breaths to bring my blood pressure back down to normal levels. It felt empowering to finally be in control of my destiny. I also felt proud to have fought for Ji to become an American citizen. A fight that was well worth it.

Three days later, Jewel, the two Defense officials, and I

made the one-hour car ride to the cemetery in Seoul. The only conversation was with Mr. Bennett, who informed me that everything was handled and Ji would fly back with us.

The rest of the ride was peaceful as Jewel, and I stared out the windows. Everyday life in Korea did not miss a beat, even with my event. Why should it? All of the citizens going about their daily lives lived under the constant threat of war, even if that war had ended 70 years ago. I wondered if all these people knew that men and women were patrolling the border every day, keeping an eye on their sworn enemy.

We pulled into a large cemetery sprawled out in the middle of the city. Our car pulled up alongside another black, official-looking government car. A man in the other vehicle hopped out and opened the back door, and Ji stepped out. She had a cast on her left arm and a white bandage on her forehead. I could see that she had been crying as she used a handkerchief to wipe away her tears. Who could blame her? She had lost her last family member and was now on her own.

As we stepped out of our car, Jewel immediately embraced Ji without any introductions. Ji instinctively seemed to recognize this stranger as both held each other tightly. They instantly formed a connection. Both women were overwhelmed with emotions and cried uncontrollably, holding nothing back. In between gasps for air, Ji spoke in Korean, pouring out unrecognizable sentences. We didn't understand the words but knew what she was saying.

Next to the two women was a newly dug, unmarked grave with fresh dirt on top. I tried to kneel using the cane I was given at the hospital, but the pain in my left leg was too unbearable.

I thought about my short time with Yu-jun and realized I wouldn't have made it without his help. He had taken a huge risk trying to save my life. Long ago, I learned that someone didn't have to wear a military uniform to be brave. Yu-jun was one of the bravest souls I had ever met.

Standing there silently, I prayed that Yu-jun's dreams could be fulfilled through his sister. At that moment, I made a solemn promise to myself—I would return to Seoul, ensuring that a name and a testament to his bravery would be placed on his gravesite.

As I stood there, lost in my thoughts, Mr. Bennett's voice broke the silence, bringing me back to the present. "It's time," he gently reminded me.

With a heavy heart, I walked over to Ji and my wife, still wrapped in arms around each other. We all stood there, our gazes fixed on the ground, trying to gather our emotions. When I sensed that we were ready, I led them to the car. We all climbed into a single vehicle. A profound loss marked our departure as we headed to the airport.

The two officials had all the paperwork, passports, and tickets in order. They even secured an interpreter to accompany Ji on the trip. An hour later, we all boarded a plane bound for San Francisco.

We were seated in First Class, a first for me during my military service. While I should have been excited, I was still reeling from the overwhelming emotions stirred up by the cemetery visit.

I was assigned a window seat with Jewel beside me, and

Ji and the interpreter were seated directly behind us. The two Defense officials occupied the two center seats to my right.

As the plane took off, I felt relief and happiness heading home. It felt as though a giant weight had been lifted off my shoulders. It wasn't how I had planned to go home a few weeks ago, but either way, I was happy.

As the airliner climbed eastbound, flying south along the DMZ, I glanced out the window and looked down at the eastern part of the Korean peninsula. I noticed a large lake to the north, the only visible lake in the area. The lake's outline brought back memories, and my hands began to shake. This was the very lake I had to navigate around to escape. It seemed so close, yet so far away. Directly below my window, I could see the DMZ line, where Heartbreak Ridge was. I made a mental note to read up on that battle's history, when I got home.

A hand gently fell onto mine as Jewel asked, "Is that the area where you ejected?" I stared at the seat in front of me, biting my lips as a sole tear flowed down. I nodded, as all words had abandoned me.

My wife glanced between the seats to see how Ji was handling her first flight in an airplane. Smiling, she said, "Poor girl. She is gripping her seat so hard she has white knuckles." Out of the blue, Jewel said, "I think we should adopt her. Yep, she should be a part of our family now."

More tears flowed down my face as emotions took over. I squeezed Jewel's hand in comfort. Glancing back outside, I took one last look through my glassy eyes as the lake passed under the wing. Looking beyond my vision, I knew Pyongyang, the capital of North Korea, lay out there. I reminded myself that a prison there was missing an American inmate.

Twelve hours later, I was jolted awake as the landing gear touched down in the Land of the Free with the newest U.S. citizen onboard.

About the Author

Don Pickinpaugh is a retired Major and was a Lockheed U-2S instructor pilot at Beale Air Force Base in California. He also served as a T-37 instructor pilot at Reese Air Force Base, Texas. After the military, he was a commercial airline pilot for 20 years. He has over 7,500 flying hours in U-2s, T-38s, T-37s, DC-8s, and A-300s. He is married to the former Sherri Juall of East Lansing, Michigan. His previous books are Flight of the Dragon Lady, Pilots of Valor, The Passion of Paul, Financial Decisions in Life, and 15 Little Indians.

Made in the USA
Columbia, SC
21 July 2024